Learning to Teach:
A Critical Approach to Field Experiences

Learning to Teach:
A Critical Approach to Field Experiences

Natalie G. Adams
Oklahoma State University

Christine Mary Shea
Georgia Southern University

Delores D. Liston
Georgia Southern University

Bryan Deever
Georgia Southern University

 LAWRENCE ERLBAUM ASSOCIATES, PUBLISHERS

1998   Mahwah, New Jersey   London

Lawrence Erlbaum Associates, Inc., Publishers
10 Industrial Avenue
Mahwah, New Jersey 07430

Library of Congress Cataloging-in-Publication-Data

Learning to teach : a critical approach to field experiences / Natalie G. Adams . . . [et al.].
     p. cm.
   Includes bibliographical references and index.
   ISBN 0-8058-2446-4 (pbk. : alk. paper)
   1. Student teaching—United States.   2. Teachers—Training of—Social aspects—United States. 3. Observation (Educational method). 4. Critical pedagogy—United States. I. Adams, Natalie G.
   LB2157.U5L43   1997
   370'.71—DC21   97-28273
                                                              CIP

Books published by Lawrence Erlbaum Associates are printed on acid-free paper, and their bindings are chosen for strength and durability.

Printed in the United States of America
10 9 8 7 6 5 4 3 2

Contents

Section 4. The School as an Ecosystem

Section 5. After the Field Experience: Now What?

PREFACE

PURPOSE OF THE BOOK

When we began writing this book, we were all teaching at the same university in a teacher preparation program that, in many ways, was based on a traditional model of teacher education. Preservice teachers go through a series of courses containing field experiences that follow a typical progression: observation only (in the introductory course), limited participation (in the block courses), extended participation (in the practicum course), and finally 10 weeks of student teaching.

The four of us each had well-developed theoretical and philosophical frameworks for critiquing schools and we were all teaching undergraduate courses with mandatory field experiences and observations. For us the question became how to translate our feminist, critical, and constructive postmodern perspectives into practice. More specifically, how do we design field experiences that not only initiate students into the culture of schools and teaching but also foster a critical analysis of the intersections of race, class, gender, cultures, power, politics, social transformation, and schooling?

What emerged from our extended informal discussions over lunch and in the hallways was the idea for this book: a series of classroom and school-based activities, observations, and exercises designed to assist preservice teachers in creating a critical and reflective dialogue with themselves, their assigned classroom cultures, and the larger school/community environment. Rather than rely on an endless series of prepackaged worksheets and/or unreflective checklists, this text takes as its starting point the everyday lived experiences of preservice teachers. Thus, we emphasize the problematic nature and dynamics of public schooling in the United States and seek to achieve a greater awareness in the preservice teacher concerning his or her own attitudes toward, and connections with, these educational processes. In short, we ask students to be more than passive observers of classroom

techniques and strategies. As Britzman (1986) asserted, "Prospective teachers need to participate in developing critical ways of knowing with which they can interrogate school culture, the quality of students' and teachers' lives, and the particular role biography plays in understanding these dynamics" (p. 454).

Silverman (1991) articulated well both the spirit and intent of our work: (a) to create dialogue between the student and the content, (b) to present knowledge as a contested construct, (c) to present material that is original rather than encyclopedic, (d) to explore ideas within sociohistorical and political contexts, and (e) to engage the student in possibility through personal narrative. Using these five points as touchstones, we believe this text is truly unique in context and content as we position preservice teachers within a variety of analytical frameworks that require them to see the given as new. Rather than telling the students what they should see, we ask them to consider how they might see differently. We hope this text reconceptualizes the undergraduate teacher preparation field experience in a dramatic and convincing fashion.

HOW TO USE THIS BOOK

Given the diversity of field experience settings, formats, and duration, we wrote and organized this book with the intention that instructors and students would pick and choose those exercises most appropriate to their particular observation contexts and interests. Thus, the exercises are not meant to be completed sequentially. However, we do suggest that you complete some of the exercises in Section 1 prior to entering the field. These exercises are intended to provide a stimulus for wider class discussions. We also recommend saving Section 5 until the field experience has been completed.

Each exercise follows a similar format: Background, Activity, Reflective Narrative, and Related Readings. The Backgound is a short introduction that provides context for the activities. The Activity section guides the observations.

This is the "fact"-finding and data-gathering stage. The Reflective Narrative directs deeper thinking about the meaning and significance of what has been observed. The final section, Related Readings, gives a list of additional resources for further exploration of the topic.

ACKNOWLEDGMENTS

To Kate Cruickshank, we extend our deepest gratitude for the FED 251 teaching materials that she thoughtfully left for us upon her departure to Bloomington. We also thank our department chair, Dr. Jane Page, and Dr. Fred Page for sharing the manuals they developed for foundations students and student teachers. It was Dr. Jane Page's manual "A Guide to Systematic Observation for Beginning Teacher Education Students," Kate's teaching materials, and the student teaching manuals created by Dr. Fred Page that provided the initial material and inspiration for this textbook.

We also thank Naomi Silverman, our editor, for her initial enthusiasm for the project and her continuing encouragement and support that enabled us to conceptualize, reconceptualize, and complete the book in a timely manner. We thank the reviewers who helped us to articulate more clearly the intentions and perspectives in this text. Finally, we express our thanks to all the students in our FED 251 Foundations of Education classes over the past 2 years who have used and critiqued these exercises, and whose valuable insights have made this a better and more meaningful text.

REFERENCES

Britzman, D. (1986). Cultural myths in the making of a teacher: Biography and social structure in teacher education. *Harvard Educational Review, 56*(4), 454.

Silverman, N. (1991). From the ivory tower to the bottom line: An editor's perspective on college textbook publishing. In P. Altbach et al. (Eds.), *Textbooks in American society* (pp. 163–184). Albany: State University of New York Press.

INTRODUCTION

At the heart of this collection of classroom- and school-based activities, observations, and exercises, is a reconceptualization of the notion of the field experience. Typically a preservice teacher's first encounter in the field is that of the "objective" observer who sits in a classroom to observe classroom practices "neutrally." Often, students are reminded to follow rules of objective research such as the following: The observer must observe the entire sequence or event. Goals, limits, or guidelines must be set. The observation should be recorded completely and carefully, and observation must be as objective as possible. Embedded in this approach to the field experience is the assumption that if the student observer is immersed in what goes on in the field and given ample time to engage in a series of classroom observations, then he or she will emerge from the experience with some form of truth about the real world of teachers, learners, the nature of knowledge and the subject matter, and classroom life.

Our text, however, aims to disrupt this conception of teacher education and field experiences. Rather, this text is intended to assist you, the preservice teacher, in taking a critical look at schools and the politics of schooling through the creation of a reflective dialogue among yourself, your assigned classroom, and the larger school environment. We emphasize the problematic nature and dynamics of public schooling and seek to encourage in you a greater awareness concerning your attitudes toward and connections with these educational processes.

Perhaps you are asking yourself: What does it mean to examine classrooms and schooling critically? We use the word "critical" in a very specific way. To be *critical* about schools means to bring to the forefront issues of power, politics, equity, and equality. It means raising questions about the relationship between schools and the social and cultural reproduction of social classes, gender roles, and racial and ethnic prejudice. It means

emphasizing the historical, social, political, and cultural factors responsible for shaping our present forms of schooling. It is important to remember that thinking critically about schools does not necessarily mean criticizing or being negative.

By asking you to analyze critically the intersections of race, class, gender, power, knowledge, and schooling, we require that you be more than a passive observer of teaching techniques and strategies. Rather than telling you what you should see, we ask you to consider how you might see in a different way—a way that is admittedly grounded in a critical paradigm. Consequently, in some activities, we generate this context through both the background material and the questions posed in which certain points of view are supported and others are restricted or even eliminated. This is done because we believe very strongly that many issues, such as race and gender, are not solved problems of the past, but are current issues that must be dealt with today.

By framing this book within a critical paradigm, we incorporate terms and concepts, such as *hegemony*, *ideology*, and *racial stratification*, that may not be familiar to you. These terms, along with the meanings they are given in this text, are important to understand before you continue this reading or enter the field. In the following section, we provide a brief overview of some of these terms and concepts in hopes that you might begin to develop a new language for describing what you see in the schools and classrooms you observe.

SOME IMPORTANT TERMS AND CONCEPTS

In part, this book is about the connections between culture, race, social class, and gender, as well as the manner in which these intersect and intertwine within our pedagogy as teachers. Two concepts critical to such a sociocultural examination of schools and schooling are *hegemony* and *ideology*. Hegemony, a term with its origins in ancient Greece, at first described the manner in which one city-state exerted control over another through economic or political means rather than direct military occupation. In a contemporary frame, this term refers to the manner in which individuals and social groups are controlled within a democratic society by some means other than the brute force of the military or police apparatus.[1] There are three players in this process that we now consider: social practices, social forms, and social structures.

Social practices are outward forms of social expression found in words and language, gestures and rituals, and the various actions in which we daily engage within our social communities. One way of controlling individuals is to define what are acceptable and unacceptable social practices. In schools, a tremendous amount of time and energy is spent inducting young persons into those social practices considered appropriate in contemporary society. One might consider asking, however, *whose* definitions of "appropriate" drive this teaching, *how* these lessons become embedded in both the curriculum and the daily routines of school life, and *why* these social practices go relatively unchallenged.

Social practices are regulated through the *social forms* and *social structures* of a society. These are the formal arrangements of laws (social forms) and informal arrangements of common wisdom (social structures) that sanction certain social practices and not others. Schools are one of the principle sites where youth are taught what social practices represent "normal" life. Whereas social forms are visible and codified, social structures are those less-discernible constructions that limit individual life. These appear to be naturally occurring divisions beyond the control of the individual. In the United States, for instance, we speak of a "class structure," even though this country is purportedly egalitarian offering no one the rank and title of royalty. We assume, however, that these social divisions do exist and that we all reside somewhere on this socioeconomic landscape with little or no control over what defines the various class positions. This belief, however, limits the actions we perceive to be available to us. The same situation exists for

other social structures such as those of race and gender. What does all this have to do with education? Schools are one of the primary sites for teaching youth to believe in both the existence and the "inherent rightness" of social structures.

Social practices, forms, and structures serve to organize and sanction social actions. The knowledge, ideas, values, and beliefs produced and reproduced within these arrangements are what we refer to as *ideology*. Simply put, ideology is the assumed right way of seeing the world. As these ideas and practices become intertwined and embedded in our daily lives, we come to accept many things simply as commonsense truth. As a social form, for example, the laws of most states restrict the social practice of marriage to heterosexual unions. Ideology supports those laws by generally defining homosexuality as "deviant."

In another example, the belief that Caucasians are genetically superior to other races was an ideological "truth" that guided social life for generations in this country. For example, at one time it was commonly known "fact" that African Americans were intellectually inferior to European Americans because of a difference in the average male skull size.[2] On the basis of this (and other) racist ideology, laws were enacted to limit and deny the constitutional rights of African-American citizens of this country, and separate and unequal school systems were established and perpetuated to accommodate the "intellectual and psychological differences of the races."[3]

Another subtle manifestation of ideology is the way in which certain words become embedded in our public discourse while serving to limit and restrict (or even segregate) portions of the population. The word "ethnic" has come to be applied solely to persons of color. In this sense, ethnic issues are understood to be those issues of concern only to particular minorities. However, we all have ethnic histories. The inaccurate belief that European Americans are not ethnic serves to segregate one portion of the population from another and sets the European tradition up as the normal backdrop against which other "ethnic" perspectives are displayed.[4] Using the metaphor of computer software, ideology positions European ethnicity as the default setting. Everything else is different.

The same can be said of gender. In contemporary society, "gender issues" are those perceived to be of interest only to women and feminists. Gender studies programs at colleges and universities usually are understood as being reserved for women. Issues relating specifically to men are not regarded as gender issues. Of course, we are all gendered individuals, but ideology positions the masculine as the default setting—the marker of normality.

Ideological beliefs exist at multiple levels in our society—at both macro and micro levels. A dominant ideology is the beliefs and values accepted and shared by the majority of individuals in a community/society (or at least that group holding power and privilege). An ideology of schooling, then, includes those beliefs and values accepted by education workers and students as the commonsense approach to the daily practice of "doing school." Consider the following "facts": There is always a right answer; intelligence can be measured; and human development always occurs in discrete and regulated stages.[5]

What impact do these concepts have on our daily work as teachers? One primary effect of ideology is the manner in which it influences our pedagogy. More than teaching methods or techniques, pedagogy is the integrated package of what we teachers do as mediated through ideological beliefs. Some mistakenly equate pedagogy with method, but this is only one small portion of the whole. *Pedagogy* includes our teaching strategies and techniques; our beliefs, values, and personal assumptions about the world; and what we believe to be the reasons and purposes of schooling. Pedagogy speaks to the entire constellation of who we are and what we do as teachers. All of this is informed, in turn, by our personal perspectives (influenced by ideology) and the sum of our identities. Driven by our cultural understandings of the world, these identities are constituted by the multiple intersections of our race, social class, and gendered selves. These are all primary aspects of the culturally constructed self.

Another effect of ideology is on the content and construction of the school curriculum. Actually, there are several forms of curriculum operating simultaneously in any school at any given time. The overt or formal curriculum is the body of official knowledge that usually carries some kind of institutional endorsement, either from the state or the district. This formal curriculum is also an ideological document. The decisions about what is necessary to be officially educated (i.e., receive a diploma) are largely informed by ideology. Why is certain knowledge included and other knowledge excluded from the official curriculum? True, we cannot teach everything, but that still does not answer the question of why some knowledge is important and included, whereas other knowledge is less important and excluded.

This excluded knowledge is sometimes referred to as the *null curriculum*. This is the structured silence, constructed by schools, about certain issues and perspectives. The null curriculum is just as purposeful as the formal curriculum. Someone, or some group, must make a conscious decision about what to exclude from the formal curriculum: hence, in the null curriculum. These decisions are all based on our ideological and cultural beliefs about what is and is not important knowledge.

Culture is the multitude of ways in which groups and individuals both live out and make sense of the conditions as well as the social and material environs of their lives.[6] Culture is not some set of artifacts, although there are forms of cultural production such as painting, music, and dance. Rather, culture is the social practices and ideological constructions we use to make sense out of, and give order to, our worlds. People do not inhabit cultures, but live out cultural relationships. We do not put on culture as one would don an article of clothing, although clothing might be a form of cultural expression. Rather, culture is produced in the interchange between self and the world. Within this transactional dialogue, our social actions are driven by culture while those same actions simultaneously define and redefine culture in the spheres in which we circulate. Thus, culture is continually in a dynamic state of reiteration and redefinition.[7]

We must therefore acknowledge that culture is something produced in our society. In this book we examine the roles of public schools in the production and reproduction of culture. As schools interconnect with both local communities and the larger social whole, they form complex systems within which individuals circulate. As we move within these venues, we produce cultural understandings, artifacts, and meanings. Thus culture is produced by people trying to make sense of the limitations constructed by social forms and structures in contemporary society.

Public schools are one place where individuals with different cultural perspectives come together on a regular basis. At once, schools become sites of cultural interaction and contestation. However, schools do not exist as some neutral field on which these relationships are played out: Schools themselves are culturally constructed sites that perform a filtering function. By designating certain cultural beliefs and actions as acceptable and others as deviant, the schools value and devalue specific cultural perspectives. The complexity begins to arise, however, when we recognize that we, as individuals, are sophisticated intersections of multiple cultural perspectives.

We do not circulate individually in a single cultural sphere. This is far too simplistic and offers a view of culture based on some gross generalizations that may lead to severe stereotyping. For instance, what is Black culture or White culture? Do all African Americans or European Americans share the same cultural base and see the world in exactly the same way? Of course not, and neither do any of the other large social groups identified in contemporary society. As social beings we are the intersection of multiple cultural points found in our ethnicity, our social class, our sex, our gendered identities, our sexual orientation, our religion, where we live, and the like. Furthermore, these constructions are hermeneutic and change over time as we move in and out of various social settings, accumulate new experiences, and meet new people. We live out multiple cultural relations simultaneously in sophisticated sets of dynamic constructions. This is fundamentally different from viewing culture as artifacts on a museum wall.

But why are those museum artifacts somehow perceived as forms of high cultural expression and representative of serious culture? How is serious culture perceived as different from popular culture? This dichotomy of serious and popular evokes some sense of the elite versus the masses, and this is one way that cultural questions help us understand how power is produced and manifested in the wider social order. In every place there are dominant social groups who control the material and symbolic wealth of a community/society. Those groups construct cultural practices and representations that affirm their central values, interests, and concerns. These practices and representations affirm the dominant culture.

Some assert that the central purpose of formal education is to induct youth into the culture of a community/society.[8] The question then centers on whose cultural practices and representations are reproduced in the content, organization, structures, and rituals of schools? Most likely it is the cultural practices and ideological truths of the dominant group. These are the groups who many times control schools at multiple levels: school board members, faculty, administrators, state education officials, textbook writers, professors of education, and so forth. This should not be seen as some sinister plot, but rather as the result of particular social groups controlling the content and conduct of public schooling. Most of the time we believe our cultural perspectives to be the best (the result of ideology). Therefore, if one is in a position to control the content of schools, one will probably want one's own perspective to be taught to the youth of a community.

We might ask, however, if it might not be dangerous to the elite to teach the dominant culture to the masses—to throw open a door of access for all. This is the point at which the multiplicity of culture plays an important role. Members of the elite are not simply those who manifest one set of cultural practices. They also must circulate within other "correct" cultural spheres such as those of social class, race, and gender. Schools, therefore, do not teach everyone how to circulate within those dominant social groups. Rather, the intention is to teach an appreciation of and a belief in the superiority of those forms of cultural expression found in the dominant culture and, by default, the natural superiority of those dominant social groups. For example, it is not necessary for working-class students to actually understand the complexities of Mozart or even appreciate the music. It is required only that they acknowledge this form of cultural expression as surpassing others such as rock, rap, country, jazz, and the like.

Where there are dominant social groups there are also subordinate social groups and, of course, subordinate cultures, sometimes referred to as minority cultures. However, to assume that there is one culture for each minority group in this country is, again, highly simplistic. One mistake made by many is assuming that *minority* and *subordinate* indicate some inherent inferiority. This is not the case at all. These individuals and groups simply do not have the same access to the material and symbolic wealth and resources of a community/society as do members of the dominant groups. Thus "minority" and "subordinate" are quantitative terms indicating access, not qualitative terms indicating worth.

Another cultural cluster are subcultures: highly specialized subsets of either dominant or subordinate groups. Individuals who form subcultures often choose to display distinct symbols and engage in social practices that are offensive to the parent culture in order to clearly establish an identity outside and in opposition to that of the genitor.[9] Sometimes various subcultures move into mainstream prominence. In the 1960s, groups such as hippies, Black Panthers, and the American Indian Movement, to name a few, emerged to challenge the dominant culture of mainstream America. Within schools small cadres of students exist who have carved out for themselves a subculture niche. You might be intimately familiar with such groups from your own life as a student.

All cultural groups express themselves through particular forms of music, dress, food, religion, dance, and language. These practices are more or less unique and have developed from the efforts of groups to shape their lives from their surrounding material and political environment. However, it is not unusual for one group (often the dominant social group) to appropriate and introduce to the mainstream cultural forms whose origins are in subordinate cultures or sub-

cultures. One effect of this appropriation might be to redefine the original intentions of that particular cultural form. For example, rap music, appropriated from its origins in urban street culture by more mainstream artists such as Kriss-Kross and Markey Mark, has been embedded within other musical forms and styles by artists such as Madonna, Paula Abdul, and Janet Jackson. Whereas one effect is a more widespread hearing for rap artists, another is the homogenization of the form accomplished by severing the style from the cultural venue out of which it grew. Thus mainstream rap is fundamentally different from original street versions and no longer functions as an effective cultural form for that segment of our urban population.

Along with the production of culture is the concurrent deconstruction of culture. *Deculturization* is the process of stripping away a person's culture and replacing it with other cultural forms, usually those of the dominant group.[10] The "civilizing" of the children of native peoples and the "Americanization" of some immigrants to this country in the late 19th and early 20th centuries took deculturization as a primary objective. In this process, those who complied were deemed educated, whereas those who resisted were considered ignorant. Deculturization was then understood as a desirable process because the cultural perspectives of other groups were judged inferior or even dangerous to the established social order. In nearly every instance it is the dominant culture that engages in these forms of "cultural cleansing" with subordinate or minority cultures as the target of their efforts.

In contemporary society, some groups have more influence than others in the production of culture, sense, and meaning, not because their positions are superior, but because they have greater access to the avenues of public communication such as the media, advertising, and the schools. Through the process of hegemony, the ideological messages of the dominant culture are infused throughout our daily lives. The growing corporate connections and expanding technological capabilities in contemporary society offer even wider avenues for the dissemination of particular cultural perspectives. Consider, for example, what some have termed the "Disneyfication" of our culture as the Disney Corporation infiltrates our daily lives through the purchasing of commercial television networks, publishing houses, and public lands.[11]

Now let us turn our attention to three locations of cultural production investigated in this book. The first we consider is *race*, an artificial social category for the grouping of humans based on the primary physical distinction of skin color that has no basis in scientific fact.[12] This grouping is usually used as a pretext for the inequitable distribution of material and symbolic wealth, resources, justice, or freedom. The smallest natural division of living creatures is species; therefore, any subdivision beyond that is a human construction. Many people, however, confuse race with ethnicity. Race is a socially constructed division based on physical distinctions, whereas ethnicity is a group of individuals with a shared sense of peoplehood. Individuals with the same skin color do not necessarily share this sense of ethnic community.

A belief in race is nearly always accompanied by a set of normative stereotypes assigned to a particular group on the basis of their skin color. Think about the larger stereotypes in our society: Asian Americans are inherently excellent in mathematics, African Americans in sports, European Americans in advanced academics, and so on. Although these stereotypes are based on popular mythology, they have become embedded in our ideologies. A direct parallel would be to argue that all brunettes are inherently excellent in mathematics, redheads in sports, and blondes in advanced academics. This may sound silly, but these assumptions are based on exactly the same defining criteria: physical appearance.

Belief in racial characteristics fosters discriminatory practices. *Racial stratification* is the construction of human strata (in the geological sense) on the basis of skin color, which justifies unequal distribution of and inequitable access to material and symbolic wealth. In other words, the closer your group is to the top, the more you get. *Racism* is the ideology that justifies racial stratification, and *racist acts* are those actions based on racism through which racial stratification is reinforced and perpetuated. Thus, racist acts occur because people hold racist beliefs and

act on those beliefs. Those actions result in the perpetuation of racial stratification and division.

Institutional racism is the codification and bureaucratization of practices, knowledge, and values that both produce and justify the inequitable treatment of people on the basis of race. Institutional racism can occur in any social organization, even if the individuals in the institution are not themselves perpetuating racist acts. For instance, you might work in a school that tracks students through the use of tests that are prejudicial toward certain groups. This does not necessarily make you a racist, but the construction of the institutional practices around you might be racist.

The primary point is this: Although the basic assumption of race is an illusion (albeit convenient for some), the effects generated by and the actions committed in the name of race are very real and concrete parts of our daily lives. The question, then, is what roles do schools play in this process? If we teach only about getting along with one another and tolerating other races (i.e., Black history month), we fail to address the basic issue that race is an illusion in the first place. In the name of prejudice reduction, we are treating the symptoms and not the disease. Prejudice, however, should not be confused with racism although racial prejudice does exist. *Prejudice* is the irrational suspicion or hatred of an individual or group formed without an examination of that individual or group. This is not to say that exposure will guarantee a reduction in prejudicial attitudes. How many times have we heard someone refer to a person from another cultural group as "a credit to their ... "? We are all prejudiced at one time or another in our social lives. The key is to resist acting on those prejudices and to attempt overcoming our irrational fears of "the other."

The second source of cultural production is *social class*, defined through the economic and political relationships found within a given society. Class cultures are produced by individuals and groups living under constraints of income level, occupation, place of residence, and other indicators of status and social rank. Again, people do not inhabit social classes, but live out class relationships, some of which might be simultaneously dominant and subordinate. As with any cultural phenomenon, social class is generative and produces particular forms of culture that serve to define and maintain class boundaries.

Finally, there is gender. Like race, gender is another socially constructed term. In the discourse of public life many people wrongly use "sex" and "gender" interchangeably. *Sex* is the biological distinction of male or female grounded in one's role in the reproductive process. *Gender* is a set of social definitions (masculine and feminine) that are fluid and change over time. Much of the confusion occurs when individuals mistakenly attribute stereotypical gender characteristics with sexual roles: Females are genetically nurturing and dependent whereas males are genetically strong and independent. Again, this artificially constructed concept leads to concrete effects in the forms of sexism, sexual stratification, sexist acts, and institutional sexism (i.e., "the glass ceiling").

A NOTE ON OBSERVING IN CLASSROOMS

One purpose of this text is to provide you with a guide to help structure observations and field experiences in schools. In some ways, familiarity with classrooms hinders observation. Because each of us has spent quite a lot of time in classrooms already, our tendency is to continue the activities familiar to us. That is, we have been students in classrooms for at least a dozen years. We are accustomed to sitting quietly at our desks, paying attention to the teacher, noticing things other students are doing (e.g., talking, passing notes, taking notes, etc.), but trying not to let these activities distract us from learning the subject matter. Thus our tendency is to focus our attention on the content the instructor is teaching. As students, the content was our most important focus, and noticing other things was a distraction.

During the field experience/observation, the major focus of attention needs to shift. No longer is content the main focus. Here, the content or subject matter may become a distraction. When the teacher writes something on the board, this is not a signal to put it in your notebook. Instead,

during this type of observation, you may find a variety of aspects important. For example, you may note the type of material the teacher puts on the board. Is it a summary of main points, key words, or vocabulary, or is it a student's name singled out for praise or reprimand? In contrast, your observation might focus more on how students respond to the teacher as he or she writes on the board. For example, do they duplicate the information on the board in their notes, or do they take the opportunity to engage in other activities? Your observation may need to account for both of these aspects.

The exercises in this book provide you with a guide to help focus your attention away from the content or course material of a classroom and toward what is happening in the classroom and why. Why is the classroom organized as it is? Why is the teacher standing in a particular location? Why does the teacher move around at some times and not at others? Assuming that schools reflect society, how is society reflected by the school/classroom you are observing? Some of these questions might produce tension as you watch the teacher doing things with which you might not agree. This is healthy. This tension is an indicator that you are aware of the multiple layers of meaning and interaction occurring in the classroom. Such awareness can only be an asset in your later work.

Some of the exercises focus on schools in broad terms and address larger questions; others focus on specific interactions in particular classroom situations. Our goal is to provide a framework for activity that helps you address these and other questions. Finally, because schools are not neat little compartments of interaction, there is some overlap between certain exercises (e.g., dress codes and regulating the body). This overlap is not a weakness or repetition, because we are asking you to look at the same phenomenon from more than one perspective.

You will notice that the text is organized around the following five themes:

1. Preobservational activities: The exploration of self
2. Regulation of the "schooled" body

3. Pedagogy and school cultures: Issues of race, class, and gender
4. The school as an ecosystem
5. After the field experience: Now what?

Section 1 takes as its starting point the everyday lived experiences of preservice teachers. In section 2, the focus is on questioning how policies and practices of schools may operate to control what constitutes appropriate raced, gendered, classed, and sexualized student and teacher bodies. Section 3 examines the critical aspects of classroom structures, teaching, and learning. Section 4 illuminates some of the competing metaphors that underlie the organizational culture of public schools. Section 5 challenges students to redesign aspects of schools, schooling, and teacher education.

It is our hope that this book encourages you to engage in critical observations of and reflections on your field experiences including the production of personal narratives and an understanding that the work of education exists at multiple (and sometimes contradictory) levels of meaning.

NOTES

[1] McLaren, P. (1989). *Life in schools*. New York: Longman.

[2] Gould, S. J. (1981). *The mismeasure of man*. New York: W. W. Norton.

[3] Stell v. Savannah-Chatham, 22D F. Suppl. 667 (S.D. Ga. 1963).

[4] Roman, L. G. (1993). White is a color/white defensiveness, postmodernism, and anti-racist pedagogy. In C. McCarthy & W. Crichelow (Eds.), *Race, identity, and representation in education* (pp. xx–xx). New York: Routledge.

[5] See Cornbleth, C. (1987). The persistence of myth in teacher education and teaching. In T. S. Popkewitz (Ed.), *Critical studies in teacher education: Its folklore, theory and practice*, (pp. 186–210). New York: Falmer Press.

[6] McLaren, p. 171.

[7] O Connor, T. (1989). Cultural voice and strategies for multicultural education. *Journal of Education, 17*(2), 57–74.

[8] Schubert, W. H. (1986). *Curriculum: Perspectives, paradigms, and possibility*. New York: Macmillan.

[9] McLaren, *op. cit.*

[10] Spring, J. (1994). *Deculturalization and the struggle for equality: A brief history of the education of dominated cultures in the United States*. New York: McGraw-Hill.

[11] Giroux, H. A. (1996). *Fugitive cultures: Race, violence, and youth*. pp. 89–113. New York: Routledge.

[12] deMarrais, K., & LeCompte, M. (1995). *How schools work: A sociological analysis of schooling*, 2nd ed. (p. 222). New York: Longman.

Section 1

Preobservational Activities:
The Exploration of Self

INTRODUCTION

Education has a unique position among the professional fields. Students majoring in education do not begin to study their field with a blank slate. Instead, preservice teachers enter their programs with a plethora of preconceived notions about what it means to be a teacher. Unlike the fields of architecture or electrical engineering in which students often do not come into contact with architects or engineers before choosing their major, each of us has had rich and personal experiences with a variety of teachers. Before deciding to become a teacher, each of us spent a lot of time in classrooms as students. All education majors (indeed all majors) have had the opportunity to learn a lot about the profession of teaching. We all know much of what teachers do and have witnessed several teachers practicing their art. This knowledge colors the way we perceive the profession of education as we embark on a career in the field.

Knowing so much about the schooling process can be both an advantage and a disadvantage for preservice teachers. The advantages are obvious in that education majors begin with some knowledge of their chosen profession. The disadvantages emerge as education majors discover, once the perspective of a teacher is gained, that some of their ideas about education, which developed from the vantage point of a student, are erroneous. For example, few students perceive the amount of paperwork required of the average school teacher or the hours it takes a teacher to grade papers and prepare for the next day's lessons.

Your teacher education program has been designed to help you make the transformation from student to teacher. One of the first steps in this transformation involves self-reflection and understanding. To transmit knowledge and cultural traditions (values), we must first explore ourselves to know which knowledge and values ought to be perpetuated. Thus, teachers must be reflective practitioners, and the first step in becoming a reflective practitioner is to know yourself. The family roles we take on, the personal cultures we adopt, the religious beliefs to which we adhere, the traditions and observances we celebrate, all are a part of who we are.[1] As teachers, we reflect these values through our presence in the classroom, and pass these values on to our students.

A second aspect of becoming a reflective practitioner calls for the interrogation of one's "institutional biography."[2] As students, we have participated in school rituals and routines; we have passed and failed courses. We have obeyed and disobeyed rules. We have been insiders and outsiders of groups, organizations, teams, and cliques. These collective school experiences constitute our biography. Part of the transformation from student to teacher takes place as our biography shifts in focus from the role of student to the role of teacher. In moving to the front of the classroom, beginning teachers should reflectively critique their own school experiences and resulting beliefs about education.

For this reason, we begin this book with a series of activities designed to encourage you to look closely at yourself and the beliefs you have about schools based on your prior experiences. The intention of these exercises is to encourage you in becoming more reflective first about who you are, then about how aspects of your identity contribute to and are influenced by the culture of school.

The exercise in Significant Past School Experiences invites you to remember some of your own K–12 experiences. Because many important events happen to us as we progress through school, we as teachers have a great responsibility to be aware of our power over the lives of children. In completing this exercise, you will be encouraged to remember some of your own positive and negative formative school experiences so that you can be mindful of the power teachers and peers exhibit over students. As you become a teacher, keep in mind that you will play a similar role in the lives of your students.

The exercise in Making the Familiar Strange is intended for use early in your observation period. Here you will have an opportunity to think and write about what you expect to see before you begin to observe a classroom. Then you will compare what you actually do observe with those expectations. This exercise will allow you to explore your own preconceived notions about schools and recognize what tends to stay the same, as well as innovations and changes since you were a K–12 student.

Finding a Sense of Place is an exercise intended to help you learn more about yourself through discovering your own comfort places. Knowing more about what spaces make you comfortable will enable you to create more comfortable spaces for yourself and for your future students.

The exercises in the Multicultural Self and the Prevailing Privileges focus on the topic of identity. These exercises encourage you to look at why you are the way you are. How have your gender, race, ethnicity, social class, and physical abilities contributed to your sense of self? These aspects of our identity affect the ways in which we have been treated in school and thus impact our educational and career choices. These exercises will provide you with new ways of understanding yourself in the culture of school.

MAKING THE FAMILIAR STRANGE

Background

Classrooms are familiar territory for all of us. If we have not yet been teachers, we all have been students. We all have spent a lot of time inside these classrooms observing the activities of teachers and students. Indeed, Philip Jackson has tabulated this time and estimates that the average American child spends more than 7,000 hours in classrooms by the time he or she has reached seventh grade.[3]

This experience gives us all insight into education: its dilemmas, its benefits, and its difficulties. Thus, when entering the field of preservice education, we begin with quite a bit of experience. The challenge then, when beginning formal study of education, is to "make the familiar strange."[4] At first, this familiarity may make the study of education seem redundant. Because we have all spent so many hours inside classrooms, almost everyone feels like an expert in the field of education. This is both a benefit and a hindrance.

Because of past experiences, students can easily go into observation settings with preconceived notions that remain unquestioned. In fact, it is impossible to enter the field experience without preconceived notions based on past experiences. However, unless these notions are questioned, we will have no options but to repeat the practices we observed as students, for good and for ill. Although many of these practices may be pedagogically sound, without the understanding gained through formal study, our pedagogical practices will remain ungrounded, and the education of our students will be a hit or miss

experience. The purpose of this exercise is to identify these preconceived notions so that we can begin to understand the assumptions we bring to the field experience.

Activity

In preparation for entering a classroom to observe, make a list of your expectations. What kinds of activities do you expect to observe? What are your preconceived notions of classrooms in the 1990s? How will the room look? Do you expect to see things there this time of year that you would not expect at other times? What do you expect of the teachers and students? You might want to include on this list your expectations of the layout of the room and the orientation of the classroom. Try to be specific about what you expect to find.

Then observe the class. What do you see that matches your expectations? What did you leave out of your expectations list that you need to add at this time? Are there any surprises, things you did not expect to observe? Keep track of this list as you observe the classroom for 3 or 4 days.

Reflective Narrative

Classrooms do indeed have much similarity. There are aspects that we can expect to find common to almost all classrooms. For example, most classrooms have desks for students and teachers, and students study from books and handouts. Why is it that the most comfortable chair and desk almost always belong to the teacher, whereas the little desks are occupied by students? After all, teachers are often out of their chairs moving around the room whereas students often must remain seated for long periods at a time. Why don't students have the most comfortable chairs and desks?

In spite of the similarities, a lot of diversity exists in the way classrooms are arranged and utilized. In some classrooms, the teacher's desk is at the front of the room, whereas in others it is at the back of the room. What is the significance of this seemingly small change? For further reflection, think about the ways in which these differences affect the activities of the classroom and the behavior of its participants.

Related Readings

Cornbleth, C. (1987). The persistence of myth in teacher education and teaching. In T. S. Popkewitz (Ed.), *Critical studies in teacher education: Its folklore, theory and practice* (pp. 186–210). New York: Falmer Press.

Greene, M. (1988). *Dialectic of freedom*. New York: Teachers College Press.

Jackson, P. (1994). The daily grind. In F. Mengert, K. Casey, D. Liston, D. Purpel, & H. S. Shapiro, (Eds.), *The Institution of education* (pp. 23–40). Needham Heights, MA: Simon & Schuster.

McLaren, P. (1989). *Life in schools: An introduction to critical pedagogy in the foundations of education*. New York: Longman.

| Name ⎯⎯⎯⎯⎯⎯⎯⎯⎯⎯⎯⎯⎯⎯⎯⎯⎯⎯ Course/Section ⎯⎯⎯⎯⎯⎯⎯⎯⎯⎯⎯ |
| Observation Site ⎯⎯⎯⎯⎯⎯⎯⎯⎯⎯⎯⎯⎯⎯ Subject ⎯⎯⎯⎯⎯⎯⎯⎯⎯ |
| Date ⎯⎯⎯⎯⎯⎯⎯ Other Information ⎯⎯⎯⎯⎯⎯⎯⎯⎯⎯⎯⎯⎯⎯ |

SIGNIFICANT PAST SCHOOL EXPERIENCES

Background

From the perspective of a teacher, the daily events of a typical school day are just that—typical. Putting grades on papers, marking students present or absent, reprimanding the same students over and over for disruptive behavior, and struggling to create at least a handful of "teachable moments" during the course of a day all begin to take on a rather monotonous and routine flavor. Often, these events become routine for students as well. However, once in a while something different happens, and the life of a student is changed forever.

The power of teachers and this vulnerability of students in classrooms is often overlooked. Receiving a smiley face or a gold star on a paper may seem like a trivial, quaint, or trite happening from the perspective of an adult, but in the eyes of a child, who sees him- or herself being judged as acceptable or unacceptable, the event can loom very large. Other examples of formative experiences might include being the only Black student in the gifted program, or being labeled as learning disabled (LD).

These school experiences, both good and bad, have been formative. They often occurred without the awareness of the teacher. Nevertheless, the teacher usually played a significant role in shaping such experiences, which need not have been part of the teacher's formal lesson plan. These events might not have been a direct part of the subject matter being taught at the moment. They occurred as side effects of a particular teaching style or as part of the human interaction among students or between students and teachers.

For teachers and future teachers, these events become teaching models to emulate or avoid. Critical teacher educators have argued that if preservice teachers do not interrogate and problematize their own past schooling experiences, then as new teachers they will reproduce and perpetuate existing school practices that reflect the inequalities and prejudices in society.[5] For these reasons, this exercise encourages you to recall at least one significant experience for critical examination.

Activity

Spend some time reflecting on formative experiences you had in school (e.g., being chosen as lead star in the school play or being called on in math class and not knowing the answer). Start by making a list of these experiences. Then select one or two to explore in depth. Try to remember details of the event. How old were you? What was the subject matter being taught? Who else was in the room or on the playground? What happened and why? Why was this event important to you? What has followed from the event? As a result of this experience, how have you behaved differently? What made this experience stand out from the routine of your school experiences? Write a brief narrative about these experience(s).

Reflective Narrative

After remembering and reconstructing these events, reflect again on them from the perspective of a teacher. Was this a type of experience you would want a student in your classroom to have? If so, what could you do to make this happen? If not, what can you do to keep your students from having this experience?

Having considered this event from your perspective both as a student and as a teacher, reflect again about its broader interpretations. Generalize from your particular experience. How does this event inform you about the roles, conditions, and interpretations of schools? Is this experience limited only to schools? Might it occur in church, a shopping mall, a sporting event, alone in nature, and so on? Where does this event fit into the culture of school? Could any student share this experience, or is it unique to you personally or to those sharing your age, social class, race, and gender? What aspects of your identity went into the composition of this experience? How did the race, gender, age, and social class, of the teacher serve to generate your interpretation of the ex-

perience? How did your expectations of school bring about this experience? How are these events related to achievement, competition, self-esteem, dignity, and the human spirit?

Related Readings

Britzman, D. (1986). Cultural myths in the making of a teacher: Biography and social structure in teacher education. *Harvard Educational Review, 56*(4), 442–456.

Fordham, S. (1988). Racelessness as a factor in black students' school success: Pragmatic strategy or phyrric victory. *Harvard Educational Review, 59*(1), 54–84.

Greene, M. (1986). Perspectives and imperatives: Reflection and passion in teaching. *Journal of Curriculum and Supervision, 2*(I), 68–81.

Martin, J. R. (1985). Becoming educated: A journey of alienation or integration? *Journal of Education, 167*(3), 71–84.

FINDING A SENSE OF PLACE

Background

Self-discovery is among the most important processes in which you, as a future teacher, can be involved. You will be guiding young children and adolescents on the path toward wholeness as human beings and toward meaningful lives. For this reason, you must develop a strong sense of meaning for your own life.

The following activity is designed to help you evaluate the conditions that make you feel most comfortable.[6] Here, you will define the characteristics of environments that are important for establishing and maintaining a "sense of place" for you.

Activity

Find your favorite spot at home or on campus. Go there, sit quietly, and think of other places where you have been happy and at ease. Are they places where you have lived or visited? Are they related to happy memories from childhood? Perhaps they are neither in the home nor at school. Are these places inside, or are they outdoors?

Next, consider why you chose this place? What aspects of this spot please you and why? In your mind, move around your favorite place. Take note of the smells, colors, textures, and ambiance. These various aspects inform you of the qualities you appreciate and the kinds of spaces that make you comfortable in your world.

Reflective Narrative

Where were you sitting while on this imaginary tour? Why did you choose this spot? We all have our own special places where we feel most at peace with ourselves and the world. Wherever it is—at the kitchen table, by a window, in the loft, or in a garden hideaway—you should become aware of the unique features of your chosen space. Recognizing them will give you more insight into how you respond to the school and classroom environment in which you will be observing.

Related Readings

Aberley, D. (1993). *Boundaries of home: Mapping for local empowerment.* Philadelphia: New Society Publishers.

Day, C. (1990). *Places of the soul: Architecture and environmental design as Healing Art.* San Diego, CA: Aquarian Press.

Hiss, T. (1990). *The experience of place.* New York: Vintage Books.

LaChappelle, D. (1988). *Sacred land, sacred sex, rapture of the deep: Concerning deep ecology and celebrating life.* Durango, CO: Kaviki Press.

Nabhan, G.P., & Trimble, S. (1994). *The geography of childhood: Why children need wild places.* Boston: Beacon Press.

MULTICULTURAL SELF

Background

Culture is a term that has received a great deal of press lately. Most individuals consider culture as the artifacts produced by a group of people. Although these artifacts are representations of culture, they are not culture itself. Others define culture as something you can acquire. In this sense, culture is understood as a commodity (like a loaf of bread) that one might somehow get through study or material acquisition (such as paintings, sculpture, season tickets to the opera, or a college course). As you acquire these things, you become more "cultured." Still others understand culture as being tied to race or ethnicity. These individuals often refer to African-American, Irish, or Asian culture. According to a more contemporary reading, culture is the particular ways in which a social group lives out and makes sense of its given circumstances and conditions of life.[7]

One great confusion of culture is the belief that people are essentially monocultural, that we somehow reside in great monolithic blocks representing singular cultural perspectives based on some primary defining factor such as skin color. In this way it might make sense to assume that all Blacks see the world in one way, whereas all Whites see the world in another way, or that all women are naturally nurturing and caring, whereas all men are competitive and out of touch with their feelings. This simply is not true. In reality we are intersections of *multiple* cultural positions that simultaneously might be contradictory and mutually supportive, coherent and incoherent. Our ethnicity, georegional origin, sex, religion, social class, sexual orientation, and dominant political orientation, to name a few factors, all intersect within us as individuals (e.g., an Irish, Catholic, working-class female). To make matters more confusing, these intersections shift and change through time as we gain new experiences and reflect on old ones.

Activity

The purpose of this exercise is to explore and reflect on your own cultural intersections. Take some time to think about what and who you are as a multicultural being. It might be helpful for you to jot down a list or maybe produce some thematic web of cultural influences. After you have thoroughly investigated yourself, informally jot down how these different cultural positions color how you define your actions, preferences, prejudices, or realm of acceptable and unacceptable actions. How do these intersections work with each other? Are some contradictory, seeming to cancel one another? Are others mutually supportive? Where are these positions relative to the dominant culture within which you circulate? How might these positions influence your beliefs about teaching and the manner in which you might go about your work? After reflecting on these questions and jotting down your responses to them, write up a narrative to share with others.

Reflecƒive Narrative

Are there some positions that you found in your life with which you are uncomfortable? How do you feel about those intersections that place you in minority positions or in dominant (i.e., majority or mainstream) positions? What changes might you make? What impact might these discoveries have on your approach to teaching or where you choose to teach? How might these discoveries color your way of looking at others, especially your students? Might it make a difference to understand each individual student as a complex social being rather than within the monolithic block of students? How might the knowledge gained in this exercise aid your future work in education?

Related Readings

Banks, J. A. (1994). Transforming the mainstream curriculum. *Educational Leadership, 51*(8), 4–8.

Carothers, S. (1990). Catching sense: Learning from our mothers to be black and female. In F. Ginsberg & A. Tsing (Eds.), *Uncertain terms: Negotiating gender in American culture.* (pp. 232–247). Boston: Beacon Press.

Fordham, S., & Ogbu, J. (1986). Black students' school success: Coping with the "burden of 'acting white.'" *The Urban Review, 18*(3), 176–206.

McCarthy, C. (1990). *Race and curriculum: Social inequality and the theories and politics of difference in contemporary research and schooling.* London: Falmer Press.

Name ———————————————	Course/Section ———————————
Observation Site ———————————	Subject ———————————
Date ———————	Other Information —————————————

PREVAILING PRIVILEGES

Background

Since the Civil Rights Movement of the 1960s, great strides have been made in our society to eliminate institutional prejudices. For example, we no longer see segregated drinking fountains and restrooms for Blacks and Whites; schools have been formally desegregated; women are beginning to obtain and even gain promotions within traditionally male-dominated fields; and the phrase "equal pay for equal work" is familiar and seems reasonable to almost all Americans.

In addition, our language reflects our commitments to eradicating prejudice. We are familiar with terms such as racism, sexism, and sexual harassment—the terms used to identify oppression. Furthermore, we are becoming familiar with terms that help overcome prejudice. Terms such as multiculturalism and empowerment are now also part of our everyday educational vocabulary.

Another step, however, in the fight for equality and the end of oppression is to interrogate our own personal sites of privilege. These privileges, or unearned rights, are of many kinds. For example, the prejudice that Japanese Americans are naturally better at math makes it more likely for some teachers to place a Japanese-American student in an advanced calculus class than in a remedial math class without even looking at test scores or previously demonstrated academic ability. It is through the process of interrogation that we can begin to understand how we sometimes unknowingly perpetuate racism, oppression, and prejudice. Hopefully, through such awareness, we can become better informed agents of change. Having recognized and begun the process

of removing the oppressive and prejudicial conditions under which many Americans still struggle, we are ready to turn our attention to the advantages (privileges) some of us share.

Often these advantages are not one dimensional. Rather, they are based in and reveal the intersections of several preconceived and prejudicial notions (see Multicultural Self and Cultural Portrait exercises). Furthermore, these advantages are likely to be rooted in beliefs about gender and race or those of race and social class. Consider this example. The local basketball coach, assuming that African-American males are better basketball players, may give them an advantage in tryouts for the team.

Activity

Make a list of at least 20 privileges you now enjoy. Include things you have taken for granted and assumed you deserve. For example, as a White woman, I know I can go into just about any supermarket and my check will be accepted, often without a show of identification.

Include also privileges you have been given that you probably did not deserve (e.g., the privilege to remain ignorant of the literary contributions of people of color). Such privileges are harmful for both the privileged and those denied privilege. Consider what you are missing by not knowing the work of writers such as Carlos Fuentes, Nikki Giovanni, Terry MacMillan, Isabella Allende, Salman Rushdie, Amy Tan, and countless others who remain outside the mainstream literature curriulum of public schools.

Consider also privileges of age. What advantages do you have now that you did not have

11

before you came to college? What privileges do you perceive faculty members to have that you don't? For example, often in college towns students (or people assumed to be students) have more difficulty renting a house or apartment than people assumed to be faculty members or local people.

Reflective Narrative

Now that you have made this list, look again at the contents. Some privileges are clearly unfair advantages representing prejudicial treatment that should be eliminated. Others, however, are privileges now because they are available only to some people, but ought to be extended to everyone.

Once you have made these distinctions, you are ready to take action. Go through the list one more time. This time, for each item on your list write down one thing you can do either to help eliminate this privilege or extend it to others who are currently denied this advantage. Now, as the opportunity arises (or can be generated by you) put your ideas into action.

Related Readings

Deplit, L. (1988). The silenced dialogue: Power and pedagogy in educating other people's children. *Harvard Educational Review, 58*(3), 280–298.

Lake, R. (Medicine Grizzlybear) (September 1990). An Indian father's plea. *Teacher Magazine*, Vol. 2 (1), 20–23.

McIntosh, P. (1990 winter). White privilege: Unpacking the invisible knapsack. *Independent School, 49*, 31–36.

Steel, C. M. (April 1992). Race and the schooling of black Americans. *The Atlantic Monthly, 269*(4), 6.

West, C. (1993). *Race matters*. New York: Vintage Books.

NOTES

[1]See Gatto, J. T. (December 1993). Bitter lessons: What's wrong with American teachers. *The Sun*, 3–7. Explore the ways in which teachers "teach who they are."

[2]Britzman, D. (1986). Cultural myths in the making of a teacher: Biography and social structure in teacher education. *Harvard Educational Review*, 56(4), 442–256.

[3]Jackson, P. (1994). The daily grind. In F. Mengert, K. Casey, D. Liston, D. Purpel, & H. S. Shapiro, (Eds.), *The Institution of education* (pp. 23–40). Needham Heights, MA: Simon & Schuster.

[4]Greene, M. (1988). *Dialectic of freedom*. New York: Teachers College Press.

[5]Britzman, D. (1986). Cultural myths in the making of a teacher: Biography and social structure in teacher education. *Harvard Educational Review*, 56(4), 442–456.

[6]This exercise is adapted from David Peason, *The natural home book*. New York: Firestone Books, 1989, p. 172.

[7]See especially McLaren, P. (1989). *Life in schools: An introduction to critical pedagogy in the foundations of education*. New York: Longman.

Section 2

Regulating the "Schooled" Body

INTRODUCTION

The influx of immigrants coupled with the replacement of low-skill jobs for American youth by automation and technology left thousands of American youths unemployed by the late 19th century. Not surprisingly, schools were given the responsibility of dealing with the large number of untrained, unemployed, unschooled, and "un-American" youths, many of whom were now viewed as liabilities to society . Thus, the late 19th and early 20th centuries witnessed a major transformation in the role of schools. Educational historians have argued that three distinct agendas shaped this changing role of schools at the turn of the century: (a) the need to assimilate immigrant children into the "American" way of life, (b) the need to prepare students to be future workers in the industrial United States, and (c) the need to provide a custodial function for children, thus making schools responsible for teaching them the behavior, attitudes, and actions necessary for maintaining a cohesive social order.

The maintenance of social order mandates that members of a society share some fundamental assumptions about how a society operates and the value and place of each member in that society. Before industrialization and urbanization, it was assumed that the church, family, and community would act as the primary socialization agents for children. However, as the influence of these institutions waned in the late 19th century, schools emerged as the primary agent of socialization with the responsibility of teaching students the fundamental principles necessary for survival in the new corporate political economy. Those principles included cooperation, obedience to authority, conformity, compliance, and discipline. To assume this new role, the school was faced with a unique problem of how a small group of adults might teach a large group of socially diverse children both academic skills and the social principles necessary for survival in an increasingly competitive world.

Schools responded to this problem in a variety of ways: a de-emphasis on the individual and an emphasis on universalism (i.e., the uniform treatment of individuals as members of a collective entity); an emphasis on the physical control of bodies, time, and space (i.e., school rules, regulations, and policies controlling how students move, sit, eat, sleep, play, etc.); the development of multiple levels of supervision and bureaucratic control to regulate what constitutes "normal" behavior in school; and the separation of the school from the world outside of school .

The early-20th-century schools borrowed from industry the theory of scientific management to create schools that were efficient both in their organization and operation. This emulation is well illustrated in the following quote by Cubberly in 1916:[1]

> Our schools are, in a sense, factories in which the raw products (children) are to be shaped and fashioned into products to meet the various demands of life. The specifications for manufacturing come from the demands of twentieth century civilization, and it is the business of the school to build its pupils according to the specifications laid down. This demands good tools, specialized machinery, continuous measurement of production to see it is according to specifications, the elimination of waste in manufacture, and large variety in the output. (p. 338)

Juxtaposed against this goal of preparing students for the world of work was the school's goal of separating itself from the outside world. Ironically, schools sought to prepare students for life while removing them from life.[2] In many urban areas the philosophy of schooling that emerged by the early 20th century was that the school was a superior substitute for both families and work. This separation of the public (the school) from the private (the home) manifested itself in numerous ways from the design of school buildings[3] to the prohibition of immigrant students speaking their home language in school.

Undeniably, the schools of today closely resemble the schools of yesterday. Indeed, many would argue that schools in the 1990s continue to operate on a factory model. The student is the worker, the teacher the supervisor, the administrators the management, the school board the CEOs, and the public the stockholders of the enterprise. In most schools, bells still dictate movement. Reminiscent of the assembly line, classrooms are typically organized in straight rows that deter students from getting off task. School days are predictable with the school schedule controlling the minds and bodies of teachers and students. Additionally, many schools in the late 20th century continue to disenfranchise themselves from the worlds of parents, communities, and pressing social issues.

Living in a postindustrial world, we must wonder if this antiquated factory model is the most appropriate for schools today. If not, why do the schools of the late 20th century seem almost identical to the schools of the early 20th century? The exercises in the first section, Mapping the School, ask you to think seriously about the implications of a factory model of schooling for students in contemporary society. The Seating Arrangement and the Teacher Movement exercises raise questions about the physical structure of individual classrooms. Here you examine how the organization of the classroom microcosm affects learning. The other two exercises, The Sick Building/Classroom Syndrome and Reading the Physical Structure of the School, focus on the larger structure of the school. Here the greater educational environment is taken into account, revealing how windows (or the lack thereof), landscaping, parking lots, and ventilation systems, to name a few, affect the experiences of students in school.

The second section, Regulating the School Body, explores the policies and practices for controlling the bodies of students and teachers. Foucault[4] argued that modern institutions (e.g., the army, the school, the prison, and the hospital) function to inscribe bodies in specific ways. One result of such regulatory practices in our society is the production of docile bodies. Bartky described how these practices function in a school:

> The student, then, is enclosed within a classroom and assigned to a desk he cannot leave; his ranking in the class can be read off the position of his desk in the serially ordered and segmented space of the classroom itself. ... The student must sit upright, feet upon the floor, head erect; he may not slouch or fidget; his animate body is brought into a fixed correlation with the inanimate desk.[5] (p. 64)

Because a large number of students must be controlled by a small number of adults, crowd control becomes an unstated goal of most schools. Consequently, schools adopt certain policies and procedures for regulating student movement and talk. Walking to the cafeteria in a straight line, using the restroom only at specified times, and raising your hand to talk in class are all examples of how schools assume the power to regulate students' bodies. Such regulation of movement and talk is not restricted just to the students at a school, for teachers are often subjected to similar forms of regulation and surveillance. For example, teachers may eat, drink, and use the restroom only at certain times and may not have access to outside communication during the work day.

In addition to the overt strategies employed in school to control movement and speech, the bodies of both teachers and students also are regulated by "micropractices of regulation."[6] These are the unstated, often subtle regulatory practices (e.g., teacher talk, classroom dynamics, differentiated enforcement of rules, formal and informal rewards) that shape what constitutes appropriate classed, raced, gendered, and age-related behavior. For example, certain practices (e.g., the absence in sex education classes of the topic of female sexual desire) operate at school either to control or dismiss female sexuality.

Other micropractices of regulation (e.g., the assumption that couples who attend a school dance will be of the opposite sex) may send powerful antihomosexual messages.

The first two exercises in this section, Regulating the Female Body and Regulating the Male Body, explore the regulatory practices in schools that seek to normalize what constitutes appropriate gendered behavior. The next exercise, Regulating the Teacher Body, looks at how teachers also are subjected to policies of regulation. The fourth exercise, Compulsory Heterosexuality in Schools, examines how schools enforce the code of heterosexuality. The last exercise, Dress Codes, redirects attention to how schools literally control the bodies of students through the enforcement of dress codes. The exercises in this section will help you gain the distance necessary to view the "schooled" body from a fresh (and perhaps different) perspective.

The last section, Controlling Deviancy, asks you to examine and reflect on how deviancy is defined and managed in schools today. Because a primary goal of school has been and continues to be the maintenance of a particular social order, schools operate in both implicit and explicit ways to uphold what are considered to be normative values and beliefs. However, many critics of today's schools argue that in its role as a normalization agent, school is an inherently hostile place for those students and teachers who do not share the values and beliefs of White, Protestant, middle-class society. Often, students who deviate

from these norms are labeled by their school as being abnormal, deviant, or at risk. For example, girls who engage in physical fighting are often treated much more harshly than boys who fight because these girls are perceived as exhibiting abnormal feminine behavior. In many schools, parents who object to the daily ritual of prayers being said on the intercom are viewed by teachers and administrators as troublemakers.

Undeniably, schools devote much of their time and energy to controlling deviant behavior. Typically, at schools, deviancy of any kind is not acceptable: It wreaks havoc on the school's managerial insistence on compliance and control. Thus, schools enact certain policies, practices, and punishments seeking to ensure that students will act in "normal" ways. Of course, many students resist the school's attempt to prescribe what is considered normative behavior.

The first exercise, Rituals of Schooling, provides you a framework for exploring how the daily rituals of an entire school (e.g., pep rallies every Friday at 3 p.m.) and of individual classrooms function to define what constitutes appropriate behavior in school. The second exercise, Fighting Violence, asks you to look at how schools have responded to the alarming (and contradictory) reports about violence in schools. The last two exercises, Taking Control of the Classroom and School Punishment, allow you the opportunity to examine the elaborate system for disciplining and punishing students at your host school.

SEATING ARRANGEMENTS*

Background

According to the educational historian, Larry Cuban,[7] a major change that occurred in the organization of American classrooms during the 20th century was the acquisition of movable desks, chairs, and tables. However, despite the pleas of educational reformers from John Dewey to Theodore Sizer to eliminate seating by rows (thereby encouraging group-centered learning), the most prevalent classroom configuration continues to be desks neatly aligned in rows facing the front and the teacher. Although many teachers adopt this spatial arrangement simply because "it's the way classrooms have always been," the message behind such a configuration clearly indicates that teachers are to be in control (they look down on their students sitting in chairs) and students are to be docile, quiet, compliant, and still as they look up to the teacher who will direct their movement as well as their thoughts.

Activity

1. Diagram the seating arrangements for the students and teacher. On the same diagram, provide additional details on other seating available in the classroom (e.g., time-out chair). Use a code to label the items: A—student chairs, B—teacher desk, and so on. Indicate the race and gender of the students on the diagram:

W—White;
B—Black;
H—Hispanic;
M—male;
F—female.

2. Ask the teacher how he or she makes decisions about where students will sit or what learning stations students will visit. Do they sit alphabetically? Are they allowed to sit wherever they please? Do they change seating arrangements periodically?

3. In observing the class, pay attention to patterns of students' response according to where they are placed. For example, who participates most in class discussions and activities: the students in the front or those in the back? Do the students who sit in designated time-out areas contribute to classroom discussions?

Reflective Narrative

The organization of the physical space in a classroom implicitly promotes certain values (e.g., individuation and competition). What values are being promoted in this classroom?

Consider the following questions in formulating your response:

What features in this classroom arrangement of space enhance learning? What kind of learning does this room arrangement most promote: teacher centered, small group, large group, individualized work? Where did the teacher place his or her desk? Why? For control? Privacy? Availability?

---

*Adapted from Page, Page, & Hawk (1977). *A guide to systematic observation for beginning teacher education students.* Statesboro, GA: Georgia Southern University, College of Education. Mimeographed copies.

Do certain students seem more comfortable about approaching the teacher's desk? Why do you think this is the case? What might the teacher do to make him- or herself more available to all students?

Do you notice any patterns in the seating arrangement based on gender, race, or ability level? Is there any informal grouping that appears to be developing in the classroom by race, gender, or ability regardless of seating arrangements?

How does the physical arrangement of this classroom regulate the bodies of the students?

Related Readings

Dodson-Gray, E. (1994). Culture of separated Desks. In F. Mengert, K. Casey, D. Liston, D. Purpel, & H. S. Shapiro (Eds.), *The institution of education* (pp. 183–190). Needham Heights, MA: Simon & Schuster.

Hastings, N. (1995). Desks and tables: The effects of seating arrangements on task engagement in primary classrooms. *Educational Research*, *37*(3), 2–14.

Mayher, J., & Brause, R. (1986). Learning through teaching: Is your classroom like your grandmother's? *Language Arts*, *63*(6), 617–620.

THE SICK BUILDING/CLASSROOM SYNDROME:
OBSERVING CLASSROOM DESIGN AND CLIMATE FACTORS

Background

Recently, workers in large office buildings, shopping malls, and suburban corporate complexes have begun to report a disturbing pattern of physical ailments including headaches, fatigue, sleeplessness, eye and nose irritation, dry throat, general loss of concentration, and nausea. Follow-up studies monitoring the indoor air of these environments have found a complex mixture of pollutants including formaldehyde vapors, radon gas, carbon monoxide, sulphur dioxide, ozone, asbestos fibers, and tobacco smoke in addition to lead in old water pipes and paint. Further research identified additional factors thought to contribute to worker fatigue and other work-related illnesses including fluorescent lighting, air that is too humid or overly dry, a buildup of positive ions, a lack of individualized control over one's personal environmental space, excessive room temperatures, closed ventilation systems, high noise levels, and poor window placement and design. This problem of indoor pollution labeled as "the sick building syndrome" is causing unforeseen and increasing dangers to our health and environment.[9]

This sick building syndrome also is found in many schools. Most modern school buildings are sterile places filled with mass-produced objects often composed of and cleaned with dangerous toxic chemicals. The rugs, furniture, and wall insulation found in many schools typically are constructed of synthetic materials. Furthermore, it is not uncommon in schools to have classrooms with no windows, sealed circulating systems, and air conditioners that recirculate this polluted, toxic air for days. School bathrooms often do not provide either cleanliness or adequate privacy.

Activity

The purpose of this exercise is to identify potential problems or symptoms associated with the sick building syndrome.

1. Draw a diagram of the classroom with its climatic features, giving special attention to the following:

a. Lighting (Natural and inside? Shades? Flourescent?)
b. Room temperature (In degrees if possible)
c. Ventilation system (e.g., Cross-ventilation? Cooling system? Outside door?)
d. Noise levels/Carpeting (Indoor/outdoor? Kind/degree?)
e. Windows (Types? Appropriate to the climate? Cleanliness? What is the view? Window boxes? Plants? Do the windows open?)

Use a code to label the items identified (e.g., W—windows, OD—outside door, etc.) Make a map of the classroom with specific attention to its climatic features, placement, and airflow.

2. Walk through the school facility and note the placement of windows, doors, water fountains, and restroom facilities. Make notes about the temperature, noise level, and lighting throughout the school. Find out if the school has had to deal with fire safety and environmental codes. Are there repeated problems with the heating and cooling systems?

3. Walk through the restroom facilities. Are there adequate numbers of bathrooms? Do bathroom stalls for both boys and girls have doors? Are both hot and cold water provided? Are paper towels, soap, and toilet tissue available? Make notes about the smell and general cleanliness of the bathrooms. Find out how often bathrooms are thoroughly cleaned.

Reflective Narrative

What do the features and design of your host school indicate to you about the teaching–learning process? What suggestions might you offer about needed changes in lighting, room temperature, noise levels, and placement of restrooms, windows, doors, and the like that would transform the school into a healthful place for learning?

How do these features affect student learning? How do these features contribute to the dehumanization and alienation of minds and bodies? Can you think about how, in other ways, contemporary Western lifestyles are intimately bound up with the rejection and distancing of nature from our everyday lives and experiences?

Related Readings

LaChapelle, D. (1987). *Sacred land, sacred sex: Rapture of the deep.* Durango, CO: Kivaki Press.

Pearson, D. (1989). *The natural home book.* New York: Firestone Books.

Seamon, D., & Mugerauer, R. (Eds.) (1989). *Dwelling, place, and environment.* New York: Columbia University Press.

Smith, G. (1992). *Education and the environment: Learning to live with limits.* Albany, NY: SUNY Press.

READING THE PHYSICAL STRUCTURE OF THE SCHOOL

Background

A primary purpose of schools in the late 19th and early 20th centuries was to enculturate immigrants and poor Americans into the "American way of life." Consequently, schools were specifically designed to establish a separate and distinct identity from that of home and community (see Assessing Family–School Relationships exercise). Embedded in the physical layout of most schools today is the belief that the school is a sphere separate from the outside world. This is most evident in such features as classrooms with no windows and tinted doors that prevent one from seeing what is going on in the world outside the school. However, numerous other features in the design of the school send a clear message to "outsiders" (e.g., parents, community members) about their place in this separate sphere.

Activity

1. Draw a diagram of the school grounds, paying special attention to the placement of landscaping, fences, playgrounds, sidewalks, athletic fields, and so forth. Where are the windows and doors located? Does a fence surround the school? Are windows and doors tinted? Where are the parking lots for students, for faculty and staff, for visitors? Which lots have the best access to the area that contains the main office? How much area is reserved for visitor parking? Where is the playground located?

2. Sketch the layout of the main office (or wherever visitors must report). Make note of the use of counters, furniture, and office space.

Reflective Narrative

In some districts the distance between home and school manifests itself most obviously in the forced bussing of students who often attend facilities miles from their neighborhoods. However, this message that the school will be a separate sphere from the rest of the world is also made clear in numerous other ways, from the design of the building to the placement of furniture in the office to the use of space.

There exist many instances of schools that have been too successful in making the separation and now are reaching out with such programs as community partnerships. Many districts are trying to make their schools more inviting places for the larger community, yet the tension still remains between bringing the "right" people in (e.g., parents and influential businesspeople) and keeping the "wrong" people out (e.g., community members engaged in violence or drug activity).

What message does the school you are observing send to nonschool people by its physical layout? Does it most resemble a hospital, a prison, a mall, or a home? How might your host school be fundamentally redesigned so that nonschool personnel could be more involved in the schooling of children?

Related Readings

Barta, J., & Winn, T. (1996). Involving parents in creating anti-bias classrooms. *Children Today, 24*(1), 28–31.

Epstein, J. (1995). School/family/community partnerships. *Phi Delta Kappan, 76*(9), 701–712.

Strickland, R. (1994). Designing the new American school: Schools for an urban neighborhood. *Teachers College Record, 96,* 32–57.

Viadero, D. (1995). Designs for change. (Architectural students at MIT reconfigure the traditional school.) *Teacher Magazine, 6,* 19–21.

TEACHER MOVEMENT IN THE CLASSROOM*

Background

The movement of a teacher in the classroom is much less restricted than that of the students. However, like students, teachers must negotiate the movement of their bodies within a confined space and within established rules of school culture relating to appropriate and inappropriate use of the body. For example, certain schools might frown on a teacher sitting comfortably cross-legged on top of his or her desk, whereas other schools might discourage a teacher from sitting at his or her desk for more than 5 minutes.

Activity

Sketch a seating chart. During a teacher-directed discussion, use a line to show teacher movement in the class. If the teacher stays in one place for longer than 1 min, draw a circle at that spot and record the number of minutes.

Reflective Narrative

Does the teacher move but stay in front of the room (i.e., stage movement vs. boundary movement)? Does the teacher move among the students? Does the teacher's movement seem to enhance learning? Is teacher movement used for classroom control? How?

Does the teacher have physical contact with the students? What kind? What facial expressions does the teacher have; do the students have? What arm movements does the teacher use? Do they enhance or distract from learning? Is there eye-to-eye contact? Do the teacher's posture and head movements enhance learning or indicate enthusiasm?

Do students move in the classroom? For what purposes?

Related Readings

Csikszentmihalyi, M., & Csikszentmihalyi, I. (1990). *Optimal experience: Psychological studies of flow in consciousness.* New York: HarperCollins.

Miller, J. P. (1993). Movement and education (pp. 81–93.) *The holistic teacher.* Toronto, Canada: Ontario Institute for Student in Education.

Palmer, P. J. (1993). *To know as we are known: Education as a spiritual journey.* San Francisco: Harper.

Sheehan, G. (1978). *Running and being.* New York: Warner Books.

---

*Adapted from Page, Page, & Hawk (1977). *A guide to systematic observation for beginning teacher education students.* Statesboro, GA: Georgia Southern University, College of Education, mimeographed copies.

REGULATING THE FEMALE BODY

Background

Although the meritocratic rhetoric of schooling may pronounce that biological differences have no noticeable impact on the educational opportunities available to boys and girls, girls are consistently shortchanged in schools because of the cultural and social expectations that shape gender and function to regulate appropriate feminine behavior.[10] One primary way in which the school operates to define what is considered appropriate behavior is through the micropractices of regulation that control and contain femininity and female sexuality.

Activities

The following exercises are designed to interrogate the micropractices of regulation that shape normative femininity in the particular school you are observing:

1. Obtain a copy of the dress code for students. Identify those items that are female specific. What messages are being sent about how females should look and act? What are the rules governing the use of purses, makeup, brushes, hairspray, jewelry, and perfume in school?

2. Observe a sex education class or a meeting on human sexuality. Compare how male sexuality and female sexuality are being presented. Is homosexuality addressed? If so, is homosexuality discussed in male terms only or are women included in this discussion?

3. Observe students in the hall, in the cafeteria, in the gymnasium, and at a school activity (e.g., a sports event). How do female students express their femininity? Pay attention to the interactions between male and female students and between groups of females. What are the boundaries of physical contact? What contact is acceptable? Who usually initiates the contact?

4. Interview an administrator or teacher about the school's policies on fighting. Are boys who fight treated any differently than girls who fight?

Reflective Narrative

Although seemingly innocuous, various rules and practices in school transmit a powerful message to girls about the proper way to dress, act, and be a female. What particular institutional regulations did you observe operating at your host school to contain or control femininity or female sexuality?

Typically, the gender code legitimated at schools reflects the values and beliefs of its middle-class teachers and administrators. If a girl is not White and/or not middle-class, her gendered identity (as exemplified by her behavior and dress) is judged against a norm that does not necessarily reflect her own understandings of what it means to be a woman/female. Of course, adolescent females do not passively accept this dismissal of their feminine identities. How do the girls at your host school resist the school's attempts to control their femininity and female sexuality? How does such resistance cause conflict between certain students and with teachers or administrators?

Related Readings

Fine, M. (1988). Sexuality, schooling, and adolescent females: The missing discourse of desire. *Harvard Educational Review*, 58(1), 29–53.

Hudson, B. (1984). Femininity and adolescence. In A. McRobbie & M. Nava (Eds.), *Gender and generation* (pp. 31–53). London: Macmillan.

Mazer, N. (1993). *Out of control.* New York: Avon Books. (This is a young adult novel about sexual harassment.)

McLaren, P. (1982). Bein' Tough: Rituals of resistance in the culture of workingclass schoolgirls. *Canadian Women Studies, 1,* 20–24.

Tolman, D. (1994). Doing desire: Adolescent girls' struggles for/with sexuality. *Gender & Society, 8*(3), 324–342.

REGULATING THE MALE BODY

Background

Recent attention has begun to focus on how schools participate in the perpetuation of our culture's dominant code of masculinity, which suggests that boys should be tough, rational, unemotional, and aggressive. For example, Lesko[11] argued that male athletes are often pushed by their coaches and peers to participate in a sporting event even when they have serious injuries. A male player who does not "suck it up" and opts not to play is often called a wimp, a fag or a sissy. Note that these terms are deemed negative because of their association with femininity, homosexuality, or both.

Furthermore, schools send contradictory messages about what constitutes appropriate masculine behavior. Boxing, wrestling, and other contact sports are frequently glorified, as evident in the athletic trophy cases that adorn many school halls. Yet at school, boys who engage in unsanctioned physical contact (e.g., fighting, holding hands with other males) are suspended or even expelled from school.

Activities

1. Obtain a dress code. What rules deal specifically with males? (Is hair length specified for males and not for females)? Is a jewelry code specified for boys but not for girls?

2. Observe a practice session for a sport with only male players (e.g., boys' basketball) or a typical workout session in the school weight room. What messages are sent to boys about their bodies and about masculinity, femininity, and sexuality? If there is time, observe a practice session with girls only. Compare and contrast the two practices.

3. Observe recess or another time when students are at play. Compare the types of activities in which boys are participating compared to those for girls. What part do the teachers play in encouraging boys and girls either to adopt or reject traditional sex roles (e.g., does the teacher guide the female students to play at the house center and the boys at the block center?

4. Observe a sex education class or another class that deals with human reproduction. What are boys being taught about male sexual desire and responsibility? Compare and contrast what boys and girls are being taught about their own sexuality.

Reflective Narrative

Just as female students are socialized at school to be "young ladies," male students are also taught masculine behavior in various ways. Having completed the preceding activities, describe your impression of the masculinity code operating at this school. Does this code of masculinity mesh with your own understandings about what constitutes masculine behavior?

Think back on your own school experiences. Can you recall any boys (perhaps you were one) who failed to meet the ideals of masculinity promoted at school and in society at large? How would you describe the school experiences of such boys? At your host school, did you observe any boys who deviated from the masculinity code? What were the repercussions for such "deviancy" (e.g., social ostricization)?

Related Readings

Katz, J. (1995). Reconstructing masculinity in the locker room: The mentors in Violence Prevention Project. *Harvard Educational Review, 65*(2), 163–174.

Whatley, M. (1991). Raging hormones and powerful cars: The construction of men's sexuality in school sex education and popular adolescent films. In H. Giroux (Ed.), *Postmodernism, feminism, and cultural politics* (pp. 119–143) Albany, NY: SUNY Press.

Willis, P. (1977). *Learning to labor.* New York: Columbia University Press.

| Name _____ | Course/Section _____ |
| Observation Site _____ | Subject _____ |
| Date _____ Other Information _____ |

REGULATING THE TEACHER BODY

Background

In many schools teachers have little say over what they will teach because this is dictated by state or district curriculum guides, standardized tests, and teacher-proof textbooks and resources. When teaching is reduced to a technical rationalist process, teachers lose much of the control they once had over not only curricular and pedagogical issues, but also over daily practices of schooling. However, in many schools there is more at stake than simply the disempowering of teachers through the denial of curricular choices, for teachers are often denied control over their own physical space and bodies.

Activities

1. If one is available, examine a copy of the faculty dress code. Find out who created the dress code. Were teachers responsible for setting their own standards of dress?

2. What are the rules governing the use of copy machines, eating lunch, going to the restroom, working at school after hours, and so on? Are any of the teachers provided their own office space, telephones, bathrooms, study rooms? Are teachers given a key to the school? Are teachers allowed on the school premises during the weekend? May teachers take any school equipment home to work on projects?

3. Examine the faculty lounge. What is provided for the teachers? What must they bring from home? Does it invite one to spend time with one's peers, to socialize with others?

4. How are teachers rewarded and punished? What formal rewards are in place (e.g., teacher

of the year, special parking permits, merit pay, etc.)? What are the informal rewards (e.g., best classes, best duty times, district-wide committeework, etc.)? What formal punishments (e.g. dismissal, probationary status) are in place? What informal punishments are meted out (e.g., exclusion from certain social events, assignment of worst classes, lunch duty assignment)?

Reflective Narrative

Aronowitz and Giroux called for rethinking the role of teachers as that of transformative intellectuals who "take a responsible role in shaping the purposes and conditions of schooling."[12] How much responsibility do the teachers at your host school take in shaping the purposes and conditions of their own school?

Compare and contrast the work of the teachers at your host school to other professional groups (e.g., doctors, lawyers, engineers) regarding the regulation of their bodies, time, and professional autonomy. How do you account for these differences?

What structures both in the school and in society at large promote the regulation of teachers' bodies?

Related Readings

Apple, M. (1988). *Teachers and texts*. New York: Routledge & Kegan Paul.

Grumet, M. (1988). *Bitter milk: Women and teaching*. Amherst, MA: University of Massachusetts Press.

Miller, J. (1990). *Creating spaces and finding voices*. Albany, NY: SUNY Press.

COMPULSORY HETEROSEXUALITY IN SCHOOLS

Background

Compulsory heterosexuality is embedded in the stated and unstated policies and practices at most schools. Quite simply, this means that all students are expected and presumed to be heterosexual. Through the omission of homosexuality in the curriculum and the sanctioning of heterosexual practices (e.g., proms and school dances) schools typically transmit a powerful antihomosexual message. Consequently, schools are very often hostile places for many gay and lesbian youth.

Activities

1. Does your host school have an official gay and lesbian youth organization? If so, observe one of its meetings. If the school does not have an official organization, in what ways do gay and lesbian youth make themselves visible at this school?

2. Observe a sex education class or meeting on human sexuality. How is homosexuality addressed (if at all)?

3. Make a list of heterosexualized functions at the school (e.g., proms, king & queen of the valentine dance).

4. Does the school include sexual orientation in their Equal Employment Opportunity Commission (EEOC) statement?

5. What examples in curriculum materials, classroom discussion, and textbooks are based on the assumption that heterosexuality is normal (e.g., in stories about intimate relationships, are the people in the relationship ever of the same-sex)?

Reflective Narrative

The environment at most schools is often so hostile that most gay and lesbians (both students and teachers) remain closeted. Think back on your own school experiences. How were those students perceived to be gay (perhaps you were one of these students) treated by both teachers and students? Compare the school climate of your elementary and secondary schools to the climate of the college or university you attend now. In small groups, share these comparisons.

Do you agree with Reed's assertion that schools attended by gay and lesbian youth are never sexually neutral, for these students constantly experience the school "as a sexualized environment—heterosexualized and highly antihomosexualized"?[13]

Related Readings

Greene, B. (1991) *The drowning of Stephan Jones.* New York: Bantam. (young adult novel)

Harbeck, K. (1992). *Coming out of the classroom closet: Gay and lesbian teachers and curricula.* New York: Harrington Park Press.

Lankewish, V. (1992) Breaking the silence: Addressing homophobia with the color purple. In C. M. Hurlbert & S. Totten (Eds.), *Social issues in the english classroom* (pp. 219–239). Urbana, IL: National Council of Teachers of English.

Lesbian, gay, bisexual, and transgender people and education (Summer 1996). *Harvard Educational Review, 66(2).* Themed issue.

Sears, J. (1992). The impact of culture and ideology on the construction of gender and sexual identities. In J. Sears (Ed.), *Sexuality and the curriculum* (pp. 139–156). New York: Teachers College Press.

DRESS CODES

Background

Although school boards and individual schools have the right to create dress codes—both for students and teachers—these entities cannot regulate the appearance of students or teachers on the basis of popular opinion or collective perceptions. For example, a school board cannot arbitrarily enforce a dress code that prohibits males from wearing earrings simply because the school board members view such actions as abnormal masculine behavior. In fact, since *Tinker v. Des Moines School District* (1969), court cases have repeatedly upheld students' rights to dress as they please as long as their appearance does not disrupt the educational process.

However, more and more schools, especially those in urban areas, have begun to adopt rigid dress codes in an attempt to curtail violence associated with gangs and consumer violence. For example, many school districts prohibit the wearing of red or blue attire because these colors are associated with gang membership. Many schools also have prohibited the wearing of expensive jewelry and clothes (e.g., Starter jackets) because numerous students wearing such attire have been attacked (and even killed) by someone who wanted their clothes or jewelry. Some school districts (e.g., the Baltimore City School District) have adopted school uniforms.

Activities

The following activities are designed to help you examine the dress code at your host school:

1. Obtain a copy of the dress code for both teachers and students at the school and answer the following questions: What are the restrictions about hair length, facial hair, earrings, belts, shoes, sweat pants, shorts, tattoos, and jewelry? What does the dress code say about wearing clothes that advertise products such as Nike or Reebok? What does the dress code say about wearing clothes that advertise music groups and singers, tobacco products, alcoholic beverages, or drugs? What restrictions pertain specifically to the appearance of females and males? Are there any restrictions about wearing specific colors?

2. Policies regarding dress codes vary from school district to school district. In some districts, school boards are responsible for creating the dress codes. Find out who was responsible for creating the dress code at your school: the school board, the principal, the teachers, or a committee consisting of teachers, students, parents, and so forth. How might the makeup of those designing the dress code be reflected in the particulars established?

3. In recent years, more and more public schools, especially in urban areas, have begun to use uniforms. Have uniforms been adopted at this school? If so, interview a teacher or administrator to find out why uniforms were adopted. Are the uniforms mandatory? What has been the response from parents and students? What influence have uniforms had on students' behavior? If the school has not adopted a uniform policy, have uniforms been discussed recently? What precipitated such a discussion? Why were uniforms ultimately rejected?

Reflective Narrative

Despite the reasons for their creation, dress codes in many ways restrict individual expression. At the school you observed, does the dress code restrict the expression of individual identity or cultural identity? If so, in what ways? How do the codes affirm certain cultural identities?

Dress codes also often operate as a regulatory mechanism for what constitutes appropriate feminine and masculine behavior. In what ways, if any, did the school through its dress code regulate appropriate ways of looking and being for males and females? How does this dress code enforce compulsory heterosexuality?

Do students have their own informal dress codes? For example, are certain groups of students identified with a particular way of dressing? How do students demonstrate resistance to the school's attempts to regulate their individual and cultural expression through dress codes?

In the 1980s many school districts banned the Bart Simpson T-shirt, Underachiever and Proud

of It. A school district in Texas prohibited its students from wearing Doc Martens because of their association with a skinhead group. Do you think the Bart Simpson T-shirt or the Doc Martens interfered with the ability of the school to function properly? Explain. Do you think schools should have a dress code? Why or why not?

Related Readings

Alvez, A. (1994). Will dress codes save our schools? *Update on law education, 18*(2), 9–13.

LaPoint, V., Holloman, L., & Alleyne, S. (1992). The role of dress codes, uniforms in urban schools. *NASSP Bulletin, 76,* 20–26.

Schimmel, D., & Fischer, L. (1977). *The rights of parents in the education of their children.* Columbia, MD: The National Committee for Citizens in Education.

Name	Course/Section
Observation Site	Subject
Date	Other Information

RITUALS OF SCHOOLING

Background

Like other social institutions, schools and individual classrooms have their own distinct rituals comprising what is often called school culture. Pledging allegiance to the flag, observing a moment of silent meditation, and listening to morning announcements are all rituals clearly associated with schools. For many people, these rituals are so ingrained in the way schools are supposed to be, that they are given little thought. However, sometimes individuals or groups challenge such rituals (e.g., refuse to salute the flag) and by doing so are often viewed as troublemakers, liberals, or disloyal Americans. Yet the challenging of such rituals often leads to the establishment of new rituals that are more inclusive of all the student body (e.g., changing the school mascot from the Dixie Gents to the Crimson Pride).

Activities

1. What rituals begin and end the school day? What happens to students who do not participate in these rituals? Are there any rituals exclusive to one school subcultural group (i.e., boys go to the first baseball game; Blacks and Whites have their own proms, etc.)?

2. Interview a teacher to discover what other school rituals exist (e.g., a pep rally every Friday afternoon during football season, an Honors banquet at the end of every school year, graduation ceremonies). How long have these rituals existed? Has anyone ever challenged them?

3. Observe the same class period for several days. What rituals exist in this classroom (e.g., lining up for the bathroom, passing out papers, going out to recess)?

Reflective Narrative

Undeniably, some school rituals infringe on the individual rights of certain students, and some rituals (e.g., school prayer) clearly violate the Constitution of the United States. Yet, rituals also serve to create a distinct school ethos and often serve as the bridge between schools and local communities. In your host school, what rituals exist that you view as bordering on a violation of individual rights or legal mandates? What rituals exist that are unique to this school? How do the rituals serve to create a feeling of belonging and community? What part does tradition play in the continuation of these rituals? Is this positive or negative?

Related Readings

Deever, B. (1994). Living *Plessey* in the context of *Brown:* Cultural politics and the rituals of separation. *Urban Review, 26*(4), 273–288.

McLaren, P. (1986). *Schooling as a ritual performance: Toward a political economy of educational symbols and gestures.* Boston: Routledge & Kegan Paul.

Oakes, J. (1985). *Keeping track: How schools structure inequality.* New Haven, CT: Yale University Press.

FIGHTING VIOLENCE IN THE SCHOOLS

Background

Although schools typically have been viewed as safe places for students, recent statistics indicate that schools are not immune to the violence that plagues our society as a whole. According to the 1993 Harris survey,[14] 22% of students reported bringing weapons to school and one in four students reported having been victims of violence at school. Consequently, many schools have adopted a "get tough" approach to fighting violence. However, in many cases this approach has not proven to be an effective antidote to violence in schools as students and teachers continue to be victims of violence even in schools that have installed metal detectors and surveillance cameras. Consequently, more and more schools are taking a proactive approach to dealing with violence by teaching students mediation and conflict-resolution skills.

Activities

Choose at least one of the following exercises to explore how your host school has addressed the problem of violence.

1. Discover which of the following measures have been implemented to deal with the problem of violence at the school:

   _____ surveillance cameras

   _____ metal detectors

   _____ armed part-time/full-time police officers

   _____ a lock-down facility

   _____ unarmed part-time/full-time police officers

   _____ a zero tolerance policy for weapons

   _____ students' lockers/cars search

   _____ closed lunches

   _____ dress codes

   _____ conflict-resolution programs

   _____ mentoring programs

   _____ teacher–student advisory programs

   _____ values/character education

   _____ peace education

   _____ conflict-resolution skills integrated into the curriculum

   _____ guest speakers that include ex-prisoners and gang members

   _____ other: _____

2. Interview an administrator to find out the effectiveness of these measures in decreasing violence in the school.

3. Interview a student about his or her perceptions of the violence-prevention measures taken at the school. Does he or she feel safer with such measures? How effective does he or she think the measures have been?

Reflective Narrative

The typical message concerning violence that is being delivered by schools is that violence must be countered with force: Thus the phrase "fighting violence." Embedded in this ideology of fighting violence is the belief that schools can be made safer if they are made more secure. This heightened security, however, makes the schools more like prisons. By making schools "prisons" through the use of force and coercion to acquire obedience, the school plays a role in perpetuating the very attitudes against which it is supposedly fighting. Additionally, one must question how effective measures of force and coercion are in decreasing acts of violence at schools. Furthermore, such an ideology has an impact on the majority of students who are not participating in violent behavior.

What message does this school send out about violence: Violence must be countered with force or violence must be countered with an ethic of care and concern? Which philosophy do you support and why?

Some schools boast of their increased suspension, expulsion, and arrest rates since adopting get tough approaches to violence whereas others suppress this same information. What beliefs about violence support these behaviors? Does your host school present or silence such statistics? With which approach do you agree?

What alternative measures might your host school take in dealing with violence?

Related Readings

Noguera, P. (1995). Preventing and producing violence: A critical analysis of responses to school violence. *Harvard Educational Review*, *65*(2), 189–212.

Sautter, C. (1995). Standing up to violence. *Phi Delta Kappan*, *76*(5), K1–K12.

Violence in our Schools. (September 1995). *English Journal*, *84*(5), Themed issue.

TAKING CONTROL OF THE CLASSROOM: OBSERVING CLASSROOM MANAGEMENT STRATEGIES

Background

A most often cited problem of beginning teachers is insufficient knowledge about classroom management. Thus, hundreds of workshops touting the latest gimmick for dealing with discipline problems have been created and sold to school districts. However, a growing body of research suggests that many of the discipline problems occurring in schools today are related to general student boredom, regimented classes and teachers, and ineffective teaching strategies (e.g., an overreliance on lecture). Thus, teachers often have to rely on their own intuitive knowledge about how to create and maintain a supportive learning environment that minimizes discipline problems.

Activities

Participate in the following activities to examine how student behavior and classroom management is handled in the class you are observing:

1. Observing student misbehavior: Note the kinds of student behaviors that seem to be most disruptive in the classroom you are observing:

_____ Talking

_____ Shouting out answers

_____ Daydreaming

_____ Throwing things

_____ Hitting other children

_____ Verbal sparring

_____ Other: _____

_____ Other: _____

When did you see most of the misbehavior occur?

_____ At the beginning of a lesson

_____ At the beginning of the day

_____ At the end of the lesson

_____ At the end of the day

_____ During transition times

_____ After lunch/recess/bathroom breaks

_____ Other: _____

2. Observing teacher behavior: Note the different strategies the teacher used to handle behavioral problems in the classroom. Tally the number of times the teacher used the following strategies:

_____ Eye conduct and/or hand signal to a student

_____ Immediately send student to the principal's office

_____ Ignore the student's behavior

_____ Assign the student to detention

_____ Mark student's name on the board as a warning

_____ Send a note home to a parent about the student's behavior

_____ Touch a student on the shoulder or head to redirect attention

_____ Stand close to a student

_____ Provide candy or some other kind of treat or reward

_____ Provide an academic time out

_____ Verbally redirect a student's attention

_____ Use a strong verbal reprimand

_____ Assign punishment work to be
         completed at home
_____ Use public humiliation
_____ Other: _____

Reflective Narrative

On the basis of these observations, what do you conclude about how the students in this class view the teacher's authority, their own self-esteem, and general rules of appropriate classroom behavior? Try to be as specific as possible with your responses.

Do you think teachers sometimes create discipline problems? Think back on your own school experiences: Did you repeatedly exhibit inappropriate behavior in the classroom? What techniques worked best in redirecting your behavior?

Comment on the following statement: "Good teachers don't have to worry about discipline."

Related Readings

Froyen, L. (1993) *Classroom management: The reflective teacher-leader.* New York: Macmillan.

Marshall, H. H. (1990). Beyond the workplace metaphor: Toward conceptualizing the classroom as a learning setting. *Theory Into Practice, 29*(2), 94–101.

Wasicsko, M. W., & Ross, S. (1994). How to create discipline problems. *The Clearing House, 67*(5), 248–251.

SCHOOL PUNISHMENT

Background

Every school has its own way of punishing students who break school rules. Typical methods include suspension (both in-school and out-of-school), detention, corporal punishment, after-school detention, manual labor (e.g., cleaning the cafeteria), and the withholding of privileges (e.g., recess). However in many schools, inequities exist in who gets punished, why they get punished, and the type of punishment given.

According to a study conducted by the Office of Civil Rights,[15] Black students are 74% to 86% more likely to receive corporal punishment than White students and 54% to 88% more likely to be suspended from school. Furthermore, students in low ability groups are punished more often than students in high ability groups, and boys are punished more often than girls.

Activities

To learn more about the kinds of punishment used at your host school, complete at least one of the following activities:

1. Talk to a teacher or administrator to determine what punishment measures are used at this school:

_____ In-school suspension
_____ Out-of-school suspension
_____ Expulsion
_____ Detention
_____ Manual labor
_____ Time-out measures
_____ Withholding of privileges
_____ Corporal punishment
_____ Writing lines, definitions, etc.
_____ Public humiliation
_____ Rewards
_____ Denial
_____ Other: _____
_____ Silent lunch

2. Obtain a student handbook. Are the punishment measures explained clearly? For example, what wrongdoings constitute automatic suspension or expulsion?

3. Find out the statistics concerning the number of suspensions and expulsions by race and gender. Observe an in-school suspension room/time-out room. How is it organized? What are the rules? Who oversees the students? What are the demographics of the students in this room? Talk to a teacher to determine what the academic repercussions are for students who have been suspended. For example, are students able to make up work they miss during suspension?

4. Talk to an administrator to find out what part parents play in the punishment of their children. For example, does a parent personally have to bring his or her child back to school after a suspension? Are parents given choices about what kinds of punishment their child should receive?

5. What are the rules governing the use of corporal punishment? Who administers it? Does someone have to witness it? How hard can a person be paddled?

Reflective Narrative

Did you notice a correlation between race or gender and school punishment? If so, hypothesize why these differences exist. What might the punishment code at this school implicitly teach children about power and the use of power?

What is your personal philosophy about discipline and punishment? Will you (or do you) use corporal punishment with your own children? Do you think corporal punishment teaches children to be violent? Do you believe in the adage "spare the rod, spoil the child"? Does that adage have a place in schools?

Punishments such as suspension and expulsion actually have little impact in deterring most misbehavior. What alternatives might be implemented at this school to encourage more appropriate behavior?

Related Readings

Jackson, G. (1994). Promoting civility on the academic network: Crime and punishment, or the Golden Rule? *Educational Record, 75,* 29–39.

McCarthy, J. D., & Hoge, D. S. (1987). The social construction of school punishment: Racial disadvantage out of universalistic process. *Social Forces, 65*(4), 1101–1120.

Rothsein, S. (1984). *The power to punish: A social inquiry into coercion and control in urban schools.* Lanham, MD: University Press of America.

NOTES

[1] Cubberly, E. (1916). *Public school administration.* Boston: Houghton Mifflin Company, p. 338.

[2] Musgrove, F. (1964). *Youth and the social order.* Bloomington: Indiana University Press.

[3] According to Stanley Rothsein, the schools of the early 20th century were designed after the asylums prevalent at that time. See Rothsein S. (1987). The ethics of coercion: Social practices in an urban junior high school. *Urban Education, 22*(1), 53–72.

[4] Foucault, M. (1979). *Discipline and punish.* New York: Vintage Books.

[5] Bartky, S. (1990). *Femininity and domination.* New York: Routledge, p. 64.

[6] Foucault, M. (1980). *Power knowledge: Selected interviews and other writings, 1972–1977.* Sussex: Harvester Press.

[7] Cuban, L. (1984). *How teachers taught: Constancy and change in American classrooms 1890–1980.* New York: Longman.

[8] Page, Page, & Hawk (1977). *A guide to systematic observation for beginning teacher education students.* Statesboro, GA: Georgia Southern University, College of Education, mimeographed copies.

[9] Pearson, D. (1989). *The natural home book.* New York: Firestone Books.

American Association of University Women (1992). *How schools shortchange girls.* United States.

[10] Sadker, M., & Sadker, D. (1994). *Failing at fairness: How our schools cheat girls.* New York: Simon & Schuster.

[11] Page, Page, & Hawk, *op cit.*

[12] Lesko, N. (1996). *Team and nation: At play with hegemonic masculinity.* Paper presented at the annual meeting of the American Educational Research Association, New York.

[13] Aronowitz, S., & Giroux, H. (1985). *Education under siege: The conservative and radical debate over schooling.* South Hadley, MA: Bergin & Garvey Publishers, p. 126.

[14] Reed, D. (1994). *The sexualized context of American public high schools.* Paper presented at the annual meeting of the American Educational Research Association, New Orleans, Louisiana, p. 16.

[15] "Guns among young people in the U.S." 1993, *Youth Record,* Washington, DC: Youth Policy Institute. (August 3): 10.

[16] Quoted in P. Noguera (1995). Preventing and producing violence: A critical analysis of responses to school violence. *Harvard Educational Review, 65*(2), 189–212.

Section 3

Pedagogy and School Cultures: Issues of Race, Class, and Gender

INTRODUCTION

This section of the book is dedicated to exploring the multiple connections of schooling and how they affect teacher–student interactions, curriculum, the relationship of schools to the surrounding social–historical–cultural spheres, and linkages between students and the school environment. Each set of exercises is designed to make the familiar strange. Having spent most of your life in schools, these places are very familiar to you. Although this familiarity with patterns and processes of schooling can be comforting and might make your life as a student somewhat easier, it does lead to a kind of tunnel vision. After a while, policies, practices, and procedures become such a routine part of our lives that we stop asking why things are done and concentrate only on how things are done. For example, consider the following routine aspects of schooling and the accompanying questions that ask you to analyze such school experiences often taken for granted.

- If a lively classroom discussion is taking place, does that necessarily mean that all students are participating, or that all students are being treated equitably by the teacher? How about the kinds of responses given by teachers? Might there be patterns of bias that are not readily evident?
- We all know that schools teach subject content, but what about that subject content which is excluded? Does that silence send a message about the worth of that particular knowledge?
- What are the historical roots for the things we do in schools? Investigating these hidden roots might lead to surprising revelations about the cultural origins of particular practices and procedures. Knowledge about these origins might lead one to consider whether the practice or procedures still have a place in contemporary schooling.
- Is all misbehavior a form of deviance, or might it sometimes be a form of student resistance? If so, what might students be resisting?

In other sections of this book you were asked to examine your own prejudices and preconceptions. Now, do your best to look around or beyond those preconceptions, and examine schools and schooling. Approach this section with the eyes of a child and try to see schools as something completely different from what you assume them to be. We begin with an overview of the study to follow.

Cultural, Historical, and Social Contexts of Schooling

- Cultural Portrait
- Historic Linkages to Contemporary Practice

Exercises in this part of the section are designed to focus on the multiple contexts of schooling and how these affect teaching. Schools exist both in a sociocultural and sociohistorical set of contexts and we often fail to recognize the presence of either. One illusion is that teaching operates only in the here-and-now and is completely grounded in the immediate needs of the moment. Although teachers must make hundreds of nearly instantaneous decisions daily, it does not follow that those decisions exist in a social universe untouched by culture or history.

Many times we also fail to recognize other ways of seeing the world, particularly those of our students. Through the processes of ideology and hegemony, we move through the day engaging in practices that may or may not be in the best interests of our students, and ultimately our society and ourselves. The questions of why we do these things and what the implications of these practices are often go unanswered. Many times we also fail to consider how others see the world and how our practices might infringe on those visions. The exercises in this segment are designed to help you move beyond the assumptions of school life often taken for granted and see the world from a wider historic and cultural perspective.

The Hidden Curriculum: Problems and Possibilities

- Textbook Analysis
- What Counts as Knowledge?
- Moral Messages in Everyday Instruction

Hidden curriculum, a term used in educational studies for approximately the last 30 years, refers to any number and variety of practices or relationships that occur without the express knowledge of the teacher and students.[1] One might wonder how hidden aspects of schooling get hidden in the first place. It is simply because no one sees what is happening. No one thinks to look. Much of what we do in classrooms is based on unreflective thought, and our actions are often guided by assumptions taken for granted about society and people (ideology). These assumptions can create a kind of blindness. To seek out hidden curricula requires you to move beyond the blindness to engage the processes of schooling from a different perspective.

The ability to seek out hidden curricula is predicated on one's capacity to see through the fog of "common sense" and demands recognition that engaging the hidden curricula must be approached as a moral and ethical exercise. Once a hidden curriculum is uncovered, several options exist for the education worker. It might be ignored, modified by changing the practices that bring it about, abolished, or embraced.[2] The

decision to act or not to act, to modify or to celebrate, must be understood as having its roots in one's personal matrix of values. The manner in which one teacher reacts to the presence of a hidden curriculum may be vastly different from that of another due to dissimilarities in each individual's set of value beliefs. Therefore, a critical part of choosing options is to have a firm sense of one's own normative position. Simply stated, you must know what you believe and why you believe it. Then you must recognize that those beliefs are going to guide your actions in the classroom and beyond, consciously and/or unconsciously.

Understanding your beliefs and the concrete effects of those beliefs is the first step. You must then weigh out the possible consequences of your actions. Again, these consequences must be defined in terms of what you believe to be in the best interest of those involved. These consequences must be seen in terms of their concrete effects matched against other possible courses of action. In reflecting on these things, we are once more placed in a normative realm of subjective decision making. Clarity of values, purposes, and consequences are essential to this process.

Once the decision has been made, and acted on, we have the additional responsibility of monitoring the results of our actions and of modifying or amplifying, according to our ethical referents. In summary, the process of dealing with a hidden curriculum requires more than a simple awareness of its presence. We must have reflective awareness, inner vision, and a firm set of normative referents with which to guide, and ultimately, to evaluate our actions.

Thus it is with education work at large. With the pervasive presence of hidden consequences in the schooling process, nearly every decision we make must be guided by our framework of beliefs and values. To choose actions based on "objective" criteria is to beg the question and to engage in uninformed educational practice.

Teacher–Student Dialogical Processes

- Teacher Wait-Time
- Brain Compatible Classroom
- Classroom Dialogue I: Frequency

- Classroom Dialogue II: Content
- Learning Activities
- Classroom Characteristics and Climate

This segment of the section explores the multitude of dialogic interactions that occur between teachers and students in the regular classroom setting. These interactions are an embedded part of daily classroom life and simultaneously take place at multiple levels: open and covert, verbal and nonverbal, spoken and silent. The Teacher Wait-Time exercise explores the role of silence in the dialogic processes of learning, and the manner in which these structured spaces can be used (intentionally and/or unintentionally) to send powerful messages to students. The Brain Compatible Classroom exercise also explores the larger communicative context of the classroom and the manner in which this context might inhibit or advance the construction of more effective learning opportunities.

The driving concept behind these exercises is voice. By *voice* we mean the manner in which the integrated sum of our experiences, our cultural intersections, and our multiple identities come together to form our unique patterns of communicative engagement with the social and physical worlds around us. Open and equitable dialogue is critical to the establishment and perpetuation of a classroom site in which the multiple voices of all students are legitimated and nurtured. As Dewey reminded us so often, public school classrooms are the seedbeds of democracy in this country.

Part of the criteria for a successful, healthy, and democratic social community is the establishment of open and equitable dialogue in which all members have both equal access to and equitable hearings in the social conversations of that community. In the classrooms of public schools, students begin to learn how such communities are established. To some degree, the future success or failure of an equitable social order may be impacted by these early contexts in the public schools. If students learn that their voices and perspectives are both legitimate and necessary for the microcommunity of the classroom to function, they probably are more likely to carry these lessons of participation with them into the real world. However, those students whose voices and perspectives are continually silenced may be less likely to participate in the conversations of their communities and may withdraw from active citizenship in the larger social world. Widespread and systematic disenfranchisement of this sort then becomes the bane of a participatory democracy and leads to isolation and retreat from public life.

The final four exercises in this segment of the section ask you to examine the manner in which dialogue is constructed and managed in your host site. Is there an open and equitable context wherein all students may freely participate? Do all students have the same opportunities or dialogic communion? Is the classroom set up in a way that provides multiple learning opportunities and equal access to the production of knowledge and meaning? This section is about more than observing who talks to whom. It is about investigating how the roots of democratic participation are nurtured in a free society.

Students' Interests and Dilemmas

- Shadowing a Student
- Student Resistance
- Student Ridicule and Harassment

For students, schools are more than work sites or places of learning: They are the major social center of their lives. Although most educational training is concerned with the cognitive aspects of school life, there are other aspects that occur outside the classroom walls. The focus of these exercises is on beginning to see the world from the eyes of the student. You might argue that you were a student most recently and that these experiences are fresh in your mind. True, but these are your experiences. Do other students see the school world differently than you do? This is an opportunity to find out. This also is an opportunity to explore the multiple realities of schooling that get constructed by all the participants. Because a portion of student time is spent outside the direct gaze of the teacher in the classroom, it is important to recognize and consider how the actions within these temporal spaces contribute to the entire process of doing schooling.

CULTURAL PORTRAIT

Background

Diversity is one of the most pressing issues facing teachers today and probably one of the least understood and discussed. Too many times we make initial assumptions about people based on some distinguishing characteristic such as skin color, sex, age, physical ability, clothing, or the neighborhood in which they live. When we engage these stereotypes, we simultaneously (a) group many individuals into some kind of unified block because we believe they all the see the world in the same way, (b) limit our ability to see the person as an individual because we cannot get past distinguishing characteristics and all the meanings we attach to them, and (c) position the individual as *The Other*, someone who is fundamentally different from us because of some physical or social marker. One resulting problem with these assumptions is the construction of boundaries that limit our expectations of whole groups of individuals, and in the same instance, limit our own.

Activity

This exercise requires you to conduct a series of interviews with a person whom you believe is culturally different from yourself. On concluding your interviews, you should prepare a written and/or oral narrative in which you present your informant as you came to know him or her through your interactions, and present an analysis of your presuppositions concerning this individual.

Phase One: The Interview. First and foremost your informant must be guaranteed anonymity, and strict ethical considerations of human research must be followed. Your school will have specific guidelines that you should follow. You will want to take notes during this time with your informant. The use of a portable audio or video recorder would be most beneficial in capturing the entirety of the interview as well as the inflections and emotions of the informant. You must, however, follow the rules of your institution regarding this method of data gathering. At the very least, you should have written permission of the individual before using any recording medium.

You should spend time discussing such topics as (but not limited to) childhood, friends, family, goals, schooling and other forms of education, leisure activities, dating, language, church/religion, work, politics, personal points of view on contemporary issues, or any other topic your informant wishes to discuss. You are attempting to understand the world as seen through the eyes of your informant.

During your conversations, identify the cultural contexts from which this individual constructs a worldview different from your own. Your intent is to identify and clarify specific cultural perspectives that provide particular meanings for events that have occurred in this person's life. In other words, it is not sufficient simply to identify what happened to your informant; your goal is to relate how and why your informant understood those events in a particular way. For instance, your informant participated in voter registration activities during the 1960s. What did that mean to this person? Why did your informant engage in this potentially dangerous activity? What was it about that era that inspired such actions on the part of so many diverse individuals?

Phase Two: The Narrative.   Once the interviews are completed, you should produce a narrative to share with your classmates. This should be more than a simple transcription of the interview. You should present both a portrait of the informant's world and an analysis of your preconceptions. The bulk of the narrative will address your portrait of the informant and his or her world. In doing so, you must first clarify the cultural contexts central to the informant so that we might understand why the informant sees the world in this unique manner. Using excerpts from the interview material helps us to understand how the informant views the world and what factors might have led to those particular perspectives.

With limitations of space or time, you will not be able to use all the material you collected in the interview. Therefore, your responsibility is to edit the material down to a manageable amount. This edited product should be broad enough to present an adequate portrait of the individual and limited enough to provide for depth of presentation. The narrative should develop in a unified manner without digression. The closing section of the narrative should address your own subjective preconceptions concerning the informant and how these changed or were reinforced during the interview.

Reflective Narrative

Why did you label this individual as culturally different from yourself in the first place? Were these differences borne out under investigation or did the commonalties of your experiences mitigate the differences you assumed existed? Were your assumptions based on stereotypes? How has this experience changed the way you look at other people who might appear to be different from yourself? How might this exercise have an important impact on your future work as a teacher?

Related Readings

Bauman, H., & Dirksen, L. (1995). "Silence is not without voice": Including deaf culture within the multicultural curricula. *Radical Teacher, 47,* 22–24.

Danahay, M. A. (1992). Teaching autobiography as cultural critique. *Critic-College English Association, 54*(2), 8–20.

McIntosh, P. (1988). White privilege: Unpacking the invisible knapsack. *Independent School, 49*(2), 31–36.

Merriam, S. B. (1988). *Case study research in education: A qualitative approach.* San Francisco: Jossey-Bass.

Solas, J. (1992). Investigating teacher and student thinking about the process of teaching and learning using autobiography and repertory grid. *Review of Educational Research, 62*(2), 205–225.

HISTORIC LINKAGES TO CONTEMPORARY PRACTICE

Background

Everything and everyone has a history. That may sound like a simplistic statement, but amazingly we often do things in schools without any knowledge of why. Teaching is a demanding job that requires us to make hundreds of decisions in a working day. Most of the time these decisions are made in the moment, without the luxury of prior reflection. If, however, you understand the history of some practices and organizational patterns found in the school, then you might be better informed when you engage in that decision-making process. In other words it is not enough just to know what to do as a teacher: You also must know why it is done. A significant part of knowing why is understanding where things originated, why they were invented, and who ultimately benefits from these practices in the schools.

Activity

The purpose of this exercise is to help you begin to think historically about education work. Your task is to link your personal observations with historic developments in education so you can investigate specific classroom practices for their roots and causes. For instance, do the classes in this school change on a bell system? Where did this practice originate and why? Maybe you have noticed the practice of standardized testing. What are its historical roots? How about other practices such as tracking or ability grouping?

Phase One: Data Collection. You should complete this first phase while observing in the host classroom or school. The information you collect through these observations is the data pool that you will organize, analyze, and weave into a narrative account.

Because field observation is your primary method for gathering material, you should develop some form of note taking to record coherently and later organize your observations. Writing notes or using a small tape recorder are both excellent. Recording, however, is a very touchy subject for people, so make sure you have written consent from your host teacher (and others, depending on your school's requirements) before taping. You will be watching for specific practices and patterns of organization that seem to be a regular part of the school day.

Phase Two: Organization and Analysis. In the second phase of this exercise, you study the data you have gathered from the host site. Your analysis should construct some cohesive view of the practices you observed and their historic genesis. In other words, how do you understand what you saw during your observations, and where do you believe these practices originated? You might want to be very specific at this point by addressing only one or two of those practices you found to be most interesting. Go to the library or your text and research these practices. Get more than one author's perspective. Many times two or more authors provide completely different interpretations of the same event. After reading these various accounts, put together an analysis that makes sense to you. This does not mean simply quoting what others have to say. Rather, construct your interpretation based on your research.

Phase Three: The Narrative. In the final phase, you are ready to put your ideas into narrative form. In this sense you are telling a story of your experiences. You should probably begin with some background information about where you were and what you saw. The narrative should be rich with interesting examples and excerpts drawn from conversations and observed practices during your time in the field. At this point you might describe what you discovered in your research and the manner in which you believe these practices came about. It is important to remember that the reasons for initiating certain structures and practices are historically embedded. The question becomes, then, why are these things still going on today? What are the justifications? Do the same conditions and needs exist now as in the past? Have these practices and patterns of organization simply become a habitual part of school life? If so, who is benefiting from the continuation of these practices and patterns, and why should they be continued?

Reflective Narrative

Think about the practices you have investigated. Do you believe these practices should or should not be continued? Why? Maybe they should be modified; or eliminated. Explain how you think these things work within the daily realities of classroom life and what the implications of these practices are, in both the long and the short term. If you believe they should be modified or changed, explain why and make some suggestions as to how this might be accomplished. Think about teaching as a whole. How much of what we do is simply a matter of tradition?

Related Readings

Burstyn, J. N. (1987). History as image: Changing the lens. *History of Education Quarterly, 27*(2), 167–180.

Cuban, L. (1984). *How teachers taught: Constancy and change in American classrooms, 1890–1980.* New York: Longman.

Tyack, D., & Cuban, L. (1995). *Tinkering toward utopia: A century of public school reform.* Cambridge, MA: Harvard University Press.

Zinn, H. (1970). *The politics of history* Boston: Beacon Press.

TEXTBOOK ANALYSIS

Background

Studies have shown that the single force driving most classroom instruction is the textbook.[3] This is true at all levels of education from elementary through university. The textbook is the source, the "fount of truth and knowledge," unimpeachable and, presumably, accurate and neutral. The textbook is the curriculum guide: It controls our learning calendar, and dominates our approach to teaching. This probably comes as no surprise to you because you have read textbooks for years. In fact you are reading a criticism of textbooks in a textbook at this moment, and this probably seems perfectly normal. That is precisely the point. We have come to accept the overwhelmingly powerful influence of textbooks with nary a second thought. Textbooks are one of the taken-for-granted aspects of organized education in this country.

Activity

When teachers are asked to evaluate texts, they usually are given a set of guiding questions such as these: Is the reading level appropriate? Are the chapters arranged in a logical manner? Are the illustrations appropriate and interesting? Is the information accurate? Is the cover durable? are the ancillary materials complete? and so forth. These are mechanical questions. This exercise challenges you to look differently at texts.

To begin, obtain a copy of the primary text used in the classroom you are observing. If secondary texts are available, use them for comparative purposes. If a teacher's manual is available, inspect that also. Consider the following questions:

1. Where does knowledge originate? How does the textbook address this question? Does it tell students to ask the teacher or to discover for themselves? Does it challenge students to create their own knowledge or does it simply tell, transmitting knowledge to students as passive receivers?

2. Who is the authority: the book, the teacher, the student, or some combination?

3. What hidden messages are embedded in the textbook? Are there obvious gender, racial, or class-specific biases or stereotypes? This can be tricky at first, but look at stories, narratives, examples, and illustrations. These can be powerful media for transmitting particular messages to the unwitting reader.

4. Examine the table of contents. What is missing? It is not so much what knowledge is missing as what perspectives are missing?

5. What could or should have been included? What would have made this text more complete, more diverse, and more representative?

Reflective Narrative

Did you consider applying these questions to texts you are using in other classes? What about the text you are reading now? What about a "world history" text that might ignore a significant portion of the planet by focusing on western Europe? How many economic systems other than capitalism are examined?

As a teacher in your own classroom, how might you supplement the texts you examined? Using available technology (hypertext, World Wide Web, etc.), construct alternatives for traditional texts. Draw up some specific examples and discuss them with your host teacher.

Related Readings

Altbach, P. G., Kelly, G. P., Petrie, H. G., & Weis, L. (Eds.). (1991). *Textbooks in American society: Politics, policy and pedagogy*. Albany: State University of New York Press.

Apple, M. W. (1986). *Teachers and texts*. New York: Routledge & Kegan Paul.

Ball, D. L., & Feiman-Nemser, S. (1988). Using textbooks and teachers' guides: Dilemmas for beginning teachers and teacher educators. *Curriculum Inquiry, 83*(4), 401–423.

Coser, L. A., Kadushin, C., & Powell, W. W. (Eds.). (1982). *Books: The culture and commerce of publishing*. Chicago: University of Chicago Press.

Jackson, P. W., & Harouteman-Gordon, S. (Eds.). (1990). From Socrates to software: The teacher as text and the text as teacher. *Eighty-eighth yearbook of the National Society for the Study of Education, part I*. Chicago: NSSE.

| Name _____ Course/Section _____ |
| Observation Site _____ Subject _____ |
| Date _____ Other Information _____ |

WHAT COUNTS AS KNOWLEDGE?

Background

One major target for examining hidden curricula involves the source and validity of various knowledge forms. In many classrooms the text (in whatever form) is presented as the primary and ultimate source of knowledge. Typically, the knowledge presented in textbooks has its origins in a White, European view of the world. Consequently, people of color, women, and even students have begun to question the validity of what is being taught in schools.

The question "Whose knowledge gets validated in the classroom?" is an important one for preservice teachers to consider, because embedded in this question is the issue of power and authority. By defining what counts as legitimate knowledge for students, we also are declaring the most acceptable ways to see the world and of living and thinking in the world. The push for multicultural education is one effort being made to rewrite the script that dictates what counts as appropriate school knowledge. Other curriculum innovations, such as the whole language approach and the Foxfire method, recognize teachers and students as valid sources of knowledge.

Activity

Observe a classroom for several days and interview the teacher to explore the following questions:

1. Does the teacher use a textbook? If so, is the text used sequentially (chapter 1, chapter 2, chapter 3, etc.)?
2. Does the teacher use a supplementary manual?
3. Does the teacher use additional trade books? If so, obtain a copy of the reading list.
4. How does the teacher try to connect the material in the text with the lives of the students in the class? (see the Brain Compatible Classroom Exercise)
5. What opportunities exist for students to make decisions about the knowledge being offered?
6. How is the teacher held accountable for the knowledge to be covered in the course? Might this affect the manner in which he or she teaches?
7. Does the teacher follow a mandated state or district curriculum guide?

Reflective Narrative

What did you discover? Did you observe any evidence that the official knowledge is still White, male, and Eurocentric? Can you cite any evidence from your observations to indicate that schools are making changes in what counts as appropriate knowledge? Was there any evidence of multiculturalism in the curriculum? How is knowledge controlled in this classroom: Who decides what will be learned and how learning will take place? Would you agree with Shannon that over time teachers have "lost much of their responsibility ... and control of the goals and methods of instruction"?[4]

Related Readings

Adams, N. (1995). What does it mean? Exploring the myths of multicultural education. *Urban Review, 30*(1), 27–39.

Castenell, L. A. (1993). *Understanding curriculum as racial text: Representations of identity and difference in education*. Albany: State University of New York Press.

McNeil, L. M. (1980). Negotiating classroom knowledge: Beyond achievement and socialization. *Journal of Curriculum Studies*, *13*(4), 313–328.

Owen, D. (1985). *None of the above: Beyond the myth of scholastic aptitude*. Boston: Houghton-Mifflin.

Shannon, P. (1992). Commercial reading materials, a technological ideology, and the deskilling of teachers. In P. Shannon (Ed.), *Becoming political* (pp. 182–207). Portsmouth, NH: Heinemann.

Name		Course/Section
Observation Site		Subject
Date	Other Information	

MORAL MESSAGES IN EVERYDAY INSTRUCTION

Background

Continuing controversy has stimulated great public debate about the role of morals in public education. Some claim that schools should simply transmit knowledge and facts without including morals. Others seek to proselytize from their particular religious perspective and view the loss of school prayer as the demise of Western culture.

For still others, this way of framing the debate misses the mark. Indeed, these educators claim that it is impossible to teach without sending moral messages both overtly and covertly. According to these educators, every time teachers encourage, advocate, or demand that students "behave", they are teaching morals.

Activity

Using the chart in Fig. 3.1, make note of all of the moral statements in the classroom. In the first column write the teacher's comments that contain a stated or implied "should" or "ought." For example, "Raise your hand before speaking" or "Wait your turn." In the second column, write responses from students to the statements. For example, "Student raised hand while speaking, and was acknowledged by teacher" or "Student returned to desk."

At the end of your observation period, count the number of should/ought statements made by the teacher. How many of these comments were made? Next, calculate what percentage of the class time was taken up with moral messages.

Reflective Narrative

Now, look more closely at the statements you gathered from the teacher. What are the moral messages being taught? How are students being encouraged to treat one another? What place does self hold for each student? (e.g., When a student raises his or her hand and is not called on, what message does this convey for that student's self esteem? How long should a student need to wait to be recognized?)

What are the further implications of your findings? Do you agree that should/ought statements carry moral messages? On the basis of this exercise, what do you think are the moral messages being sent most often to children in public schools? Can you agree with these morals? Why or why not?

Related Readings

Beck, C. (1995). Postmodernism, ethics, and moral education. In W. Kohli (Ed.), *Critical conversations in philosophy of education* (pp. 127–36) New York: Routledge.

Noddings, N. (1992). *The challenge to care in schools: An alternative approach to education.* New York: Teachers College Press.

Purpel, D. (1989). *The moral and spiritual crisis in education: A curriculum for justice and compassion in education.* New York: Bergin & Garvey.

Comments of Teachers	Comments/Responses of Students

FIG 3.1. Moral Messages in Everyday Instruction Worksheet (reproduce as needed).

TEACHER WAIT-TIME[5]

Background

Most people believe that speech is the most effective way to communicate thoughts and ideas to others. Speaking is, in fact, the most commonly used form of communication in our society. However, what we do not say, or more specifically, the interspaces between what we do say are also powerful components of the communication process. But, like many other aspects of teaching, we neither fully realize nor explore the effects generated by this subtle nonverbal aspect of communication.

In formal training, most preservice teachers are taught the art of questioning. One part of the questioning process is *wait-time*: the time between the question and either the student response or your follow-up. Many teachers vaguely recommend some general amount of wait-time (until the student starts to get uncomfortable or is clearly perplexed), but we focus here on wait-time as a specific and powerful communicative tool that speaks through its structured silences. Embedded in wait-time are subtle clues about your judgments of a student's abilities and your expectations of individuals and groups. For example, the more time you allow a student to mull through a question, the more you trust his or her ability to answer that question without getting flustered.

As a rule, the practice of prompting is not a problem. Giving support and helping students reason through difficult conundrums is part of being an effective teacher. The problem emerges, however, if you consistently distribute wait-time inequitably. For instance, if female students are consistently given significantly less wait time than are male students, a powerful prejudicial message might be sent to the class as a whole about the perceived abilities of these individuals.

Activity

Phase One.   In Fig. 3.2 is a chart on which to record your observations about teacher wait-time. You may need a stopwatch for this exercise, although any clock that indicates seconds will be sufficient (and unobtrusive). In looking at the chart, you will notice the following nomenclature for recording your observations.

M	F	Wait Time
✓		:25
	✓	X
✓		:13

When the teacher asks a student a question, start your watch and check whether the student is female or male. If the student speaks before the teacher, place an X in the Wait-Time box. If the teacher speaks before the student, stop your watch and write down the elapsed time. Do not expect to catch every interchange, especially in classes with lively questioning and a fast pace. However, over an extended period of time, patterns will emerge.

Phase Two.   Talk with male and female students from the classes you observed and ask them how they like those particular subjects. See if they mention the teacher's attitude in their comments.

Reflective Afterthoughts

What patterns did you discover? If the teacher was equitable in his or her questioning, ask why and how questioning is part of his or her pedagogy. Are there other aspects to the class that contradict or support your wait-time observations? How might you teach yourself to be more aware of wait-time in your own teaching?

Related Readings

Freed, A. F. (1992). We understand perfectly: A critique of Tannen's view of cross-sex communication. In K. Hall, M. Bucholtz, & B. Moonwoman (Eds.), *Locating power: Proceedings of the second Berkeley women and language conference 1* (pp. 144–152). Berkeley, CA: Berkeley Women and Language Group.

McDermott, R. P. (1977). Social relations as contexts for learning in school. *Harvard Educational Review, 47*(2), 198–213.

Sadker, M., Sadker, D., & Long, L. (1989). Gender and educational equality. In J. A. Banks & C. A. M. Banks (Eds.), *Multicultural education: Issues and perspectives* (pp. 105–123). Boston: Allyn & Bacon.

Tannen, D. (1990). *You just don't understand: Men and women in conversation*. New York: Ballantine Books.

Weikel, B. (1995). "Girlspeak" and "Boyspeak": Gender differences in classroom discussion. In J. S. Kleinfeld & S. Yerian (Eds.), *Gender tales: Tensions in the schools* (pp. 7–11). New York: St. Martin's Press.

F	M	Wait Time	F	M	Wait Time	F	M	Wait Time

FIG 3.2 Wait-Time Worksheet (reproduce as needed).

BRAIN-COMPATIBLE CLASSROOM EXERCISE

Background

Recent findings in neuroscience are important for the field of education. Teachers are often so busy with the mechanics of teaching that they forget that "the brain is the organ of learning."[6] In our teacher preparation programs, we spend considerable time learning how to plan a lesson and how to deliver it but devote little or no time to learning about how the brain functions. We now know a great deal about how the brain is impacted by enriched environments, threats, food, stress, feedback, and hundreds of other stimuli, but how does it all relate to the classroom?

The brain-based or brain-compatible classroom approach is based on current research in neuroscience that suggests how our brain naturally learns best. This approach is not a panacea for all pedagogical problems, but it does provide a research-based and biologically driven framework for understanding learning. To learn better, we first must better understand the human brain.

Neurons are the basic cells of the brain. Most neurons form connections with other neurons rather than function independently and randomly. In this way the brain constructs neural networks. These networks tend to form and reform in a set order. Once a neural network is formed, it has a tendency to reform again and again. In much the same way as people at a crowded party tend to gravitate toward individuals they already know, neurons gravitate toward familiar neurons—those that have previously been in associated networks.

Findings such as these from the field of neuroscience indicate that certain classroom practices and activities should be more successful than others. The primary indication is learning occurs best when ideas are placed in context so that students can connect new learning with previously established neural networks. Thus, subject matter in schools should be relevant to real-life concerns of learners. As real-life concerns are transformed into classroom projects, the false separation between real life and classroom life dissolves, and students encounter education in an integrated fashion.

In addition to working with students' neural networks, educational practices should allow students to choose a topic, the method of addressing the topic, and the manner of demonstrating an understanding of the topic, thus feeding the students' natural *epistemic hunger* or the genetically driven imperative to form neural networks.[7] Therefore, the more students discover and simultaneously create neural networks, the more they desire to learn.

Activity

Relate these findings of neuroscience the classroom you are observing. What kinds of connections are being made between the real life of students outside the classroom and the subject matter being presented? Are narratives or stories used to enhance the students' contextual understandings of the material? In what ways does the teacher relate new learning to previous learning, thus building on preexisting neural networks? How much choice do students have in determining their studies? Are students allowed to design their own methods of presentation and evaluation?

Reflective Narrative

An important factor that influences the readiness of the human brain for learning is related to tension and stress. Stressful environments initiate "fight or flight" responses in the brain stem and inhibit the firing of neurons in the cerebrum. Knowing this, what can teachers do to reduce the tension in a classroom? Are classrooms inherently stressful for some students? How can teachers present a challenging curriculum without creating a stressful environment?

Related Readings

Cain, R., & Geoffrey, C. (1991). *Making connections: Teaching and the human brain*. Alexandria, VA: Association for Supervision of Curriculum Development.

Goleman, D. (1995). *Emotional intelligence*. New York: Bantam.

Laughlin, C. D., McMannus, J., & D'Aquilli, G. G. (1990). *Brain, symbol, & experience: Toward a neurophenomenology of human consciousness*. Boston: New Science Library.

Liston, D. D. (1995 Fall). Basic guidelines for brain-compatible classrooms. *National Association of Laboratory Schools Journal, 19*(3), 13–18.

Sylwester, R. (1995). *A celebration of neurons: An educator's guide to the human brain*. Alexandria, VA: Association for Supervision and Curriculum Development.

Name ______________________________ Course/Section ____________________

Observation Site ____________________________ Subject ____________________

Date ______________ Other Information ______________________________________

CLASSROOM DIALOGUE I: FREQUENCY[8]

Background

Dialogic interaction is one of the most intricate and complex aspects of classroom teaching. Ensuring that all students have (at the very least) opportunities to participate is an egalitarian goal that is difficult to achieve. But, partialities begin to emerge as certain students seem to be more adept at dealing with certain questions and problems. When we know which individuals are more likely to answer correctly (or at least answer), they become the anchors of our discussions. If all else fails and the exercise is grinding to a halt, we know we can look to those individuals to "bail us out" and get the discussion moving.

Activity

Observe a classroom in which formal discussions are taking place between the teacher and either the entire group or a portion of the class. Doing this exercise in three different sites (elementary, middle/junior high, and high school) would bring an additional dimension to the activity. In the space provided on the data sheet in Fig. 3.3, record your observations of the dialogue between the teacher and the class.

First, construct a matrix of the students using identifiers of sex and broad ethnic groupings. (e.g., BF—Black female; AM—Asian male; EF—European female; HM—Hispanic male; etc.). Then use a simple tally system to record the *number* of interactions between individual students and the teacher.

BF	III
AM	~~IIII~~

Reflective Afterthoughts

Did any patterns develop? Did the teacher serve as a source of encouragement or as a barrier to future participation? Were some students called on more than others? Did students seem to respond to the patterns that the teacher established? Did students who received consistent attention increase their rates of participation? Did students who were not regularly included withdraw from the discussion?

What might you as a future teacher learn from this exercise? What role might your prejudices play in your manner of constructing the dialogue in your classroom? What might you do to ensure more equitable treatment and opportunities for all your students?

Move on to Classroom Dialogue II to further explore this issue.

Related Readings

American Association of University Women. (1993). *How schools shortchange girls: A study of major findings on girls and education.* Washington, DC: Author & National Education Association.

D'Amato, J. D. (1988). "Acting": Hawaiian children's resistance to teachers. *The Elementary School Journal, 88*, 529–544.

Labov, W. (1972). *Language in the inner city: Studies in the Black English vernacular.* Philadelphia: University of Pennsylvania Press.

Leap, W. L. (1993). *American Indian English.* Salt Lake City: University of Utah Press.

Purcell-Gates, V. (1993). I ain't never read my own words before. *Journal of Reading, 37*(8), 210–219.

Identifier	Frequency	Identifier	Frequency

FIG. 3.3. Classroom Dialogue I Worksheet (reproduce as needed).

CLASSROOM DIALOGUE II: CONTENT[9]

Background

In the Classroom Dialogue I exercise, the focus was on how frequently students were called on. This exercise looks at the content of classroom interactions. Teacher responses to students can vary widely from praise, through indifference, to condemnation. The following is an investigation of teacher response patterns during classroom discussions.

Activity

Observe a classroom in which formal discussions are taking place between the teacher and either the entire group or a portion of the class. Doing this exercise in three different sites—elementary, middle/junior high, and high school—would bring an additional dimension to the activity. In the space provided on your data sheet from Fig 3.4, record your observations of the dialogue between the teacher and the class.

First, construct a matrix of the students using identifiers of sex and broad ethnic groupings (e.g., BF—Black female; AM—Asian male; EF—European female; HM—Hispanic male; etc). Then use the following nomenclature to record the content of the interactions between individual students and the teacher.

A Academic (dialogue pertains to the topic)
R Redirect (dialogue designed to bring students back toward the topic, but not a reprimand)
P Praise and/or validation (affirmation)
M Classroom Management (reprimand)

For example:

BM	BF	AM	AF	EF	EM	HF	HM
A	M	A	R	M	M	A	M
R	P	P	A	M	A	R	
P	A	A		M	M	M	

When you have completed your observations, tally the sheets and look for emerging patterns.

Reflective Afterthoughts

Did the teacher serve as a source of encouragement for all students, or as a barrier to participation for some? Were some students called on more than others? Were some students praised more than others? Were some students reprimanded more than others? Did students seem to respond to the patterns that the teacher established? Did students who received consistent praise increase their rates of participation? Did students who were regularly reprimanded withdraw from the cognitive discussion and engage in forms of resistance (including silence)?

What might you as a future teacher learn from this exercise? What role might your prejudices play in way you construct the dialogue within your own classroom? What might you do to ensure more equitable treatment and opportunities for all your students?

Related Readings

Deever, B. (1993). A curriculum for educational justice: The social foundations of education and preservice teachers. *Teacher Education Quarterly, 20*(2), 43–56.

Giroux, H. A. (1988). *Teachers as intellectuals: Toward a critical pedagogy of learning.* Hadley, MA: Bergin & Garvey.

Lappe, F. M., & DuBois, P. M. (1993). Others study democracy—We do it. *Democracy and Education,* 7(3), 9–14.

Roman, L. G. (1993). White is a color/white defensiveness, postmodernism, and anti-racist pedagogy. In C. McCarthy & W. Crichelow (Eds.), *Race, identity, and representation in education* (pp. xx–xx). New York: Routledge.

Thompson, B., & Disch, E. (1992). Feminist, anti-racist, anti-oppression teaching: Two white women's experience. *Radical Teacher, 41,* 4–10.

(A) Academic (R) Redirect (P) Praise and/or Validation (M) Classroom Management

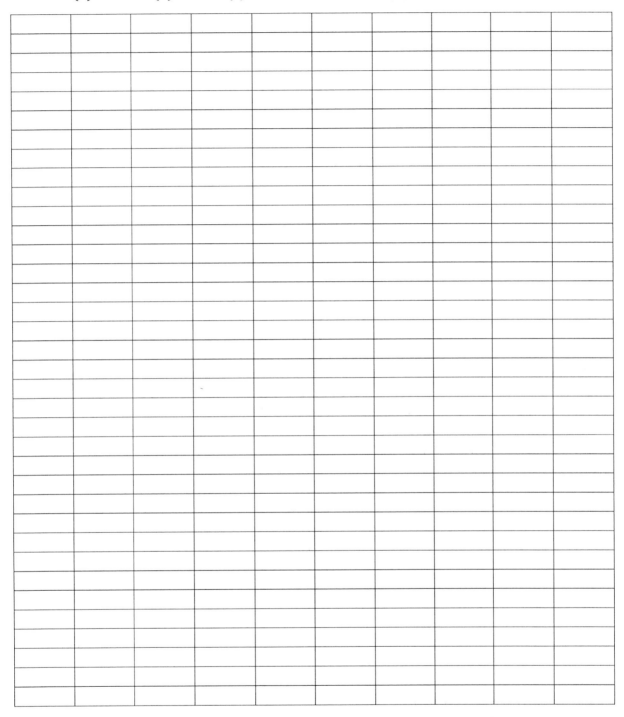

FIG 3.4. Classroom Dialogue II Worksheet (reproduce as needed).

LEARNING ACTIVITIES

Background

Part of being a teacher is planning activities for students. Embedded in the activities teachers design are hidden assumptions about students' abilities and needs. Often these assumptions are based on nonacademic criteria such as race, social class, gender, culture, and/or ethnic origin.

Activity

Observe two or more classrooms to explore the learning activities in which students are supposed to be engaged. If possible, select two classes that differ in the supposed makeup of students (e.g., a gifted class and a general class). Use the data sheet from Fig 3.5 to record your observations.

Reflective Narrative

What differences did you observe between the two classes? What do you think is the significance of these differences? Why do you think these differences exist? Might it be teaching style, course content, perceptions of students, expectations of teachers, or some combination thereof?

Related Readings

Calabrese, B. A. (1995). Oral histories: New teaching method that challenges students' misconceptions of chemistry and its relevance in everyday life. *Chemistry and Industry*, (2), 60.

Jacono, B. J., & Jacono, J. J. (1994). Holism: The teacher is the method. *Nurse Education Today*, *14*(4), 287–291.

Loughrinsacco, S. J. (1992). More than meets the eye: An ethnography of an elementary French class. *Canadian Modern Language Review—revue Canadienne Des Langues Vivantes*, *49*(1), 80–101.

Robinson, B. D., & Schaible, R. (1993). Women and men teaching men, women, and work. *Teaching Sociology*, *21*(4), 363–370.

Woods, P. (1993). Towards a theory of aesthetic learning. *Educational Studies*, *19*(3), 323–338.

Activity	Class #1	Class #2	(Class #3)	(Class #4)
Writing on the board	_____	_____	_____	_____
Note taking	_____	_____	_____	_____
Worksheets	_____	_____	_____	_____
Listening	_____	_____	_____	_____
Asking questions	_____	_____	_____	_____
Group work	_____	_____	_____	_____
Talking with one another	_____	_____	_____	_____
Computer work alone	_____	_____	_____	_____
Computer work in groups	_____	_____	_____	_____
Watching a video	_____	_____	_____	_____
Reading	_____	_____	_____	_____
"Hands-on" activities	_____	_____	_____	_____
Group discussion	_____	_____	_____	_____
Review games	_____	_____	_____	_____
Exploration games	_____	_____	_____	_____
Social games	_____	_____	_____	_____
Writing	_____	_____	_____	_____
Other _____	_____	_____	_____	_____

FIG 3.5. Learning Activities Worksheet (reproduce as needed).

CLASSROOM CHARACTERISTICS AND CLIMATE

Background

The purpose of this activity is to record and analyze the characteristics and overall climate of one or more classrooms. Five headings for characteristics have been adapted from the work of Fischer and Fischer.[10]

Task-oriented: This is the classroom in which prescribed lessons are studied by all students using the same set of resources. Each student works to meet strict preestablished goals that have been described explicitly before the lessons begin. Work time is rigidly controlled.

Cooperative: This is the classroom in which the teacher has given some control to the students regarding resources, working conditions, timetables, and the like. Although the teacher still retains control over the parameters of the lessons, he or she acts more as a facilitator.

Student-centered: This is the classroom in which the interests and curiosities of the students guide the direction of their inquiries. In this setting the subject content is secondary to student interests. The teacher's responsibilities are to support these inquiries along a very broad avenue without becoming directive.

Subject-centered: This is the classroom in which the content drives all considerations of planning and organization. The student is excluded from consideration. In this setting, the goal is to cover the material as scheduled regardless of student interest or learning.

Learning-centered: This is the classroom in which a balance is struck between student-centered and subject-centered learning. In this setting, the teacher attempts to honor a commitment both to the individual needs, experiences, and interests of the students and to the subject matter content.

There are two headings under climate that have also been adopted from Fischer and Fischer.[11]

Emotionally involved: This is the classroom in which the teacher is personally involved with the learning process as an active participant exhibiting zeal and energy. The result is usually a mix of high emotion and intense personal student involvement. These classrooms may sometimes appear chaotic at first glance.

Emotionally detached: This is the classroom in which the teacher sets a tone of dispassionate rationality. Students are challenged through a more orderly process of detached inquiry. The emotional tenor in this setting is subdued, but may still exist as a kind of unacknowledged undercurrent that emerges from time to time. This undercurrent is quickly subsumed, however, to dispassionate rationality. The learning that takes place in this setting may be no more or less significant than that which occurs in the emotionally involved classroom.

Activity

After observing two or more classes, think back to the general feelings you perceived in each classroom. On the Classroom Characteristics and Climate Work sheet from Fig. 3.6, you are asked to indicate the degree to which these teachers created particular learning climates and to assess the characteristics of their classrooms. After observing two or more classes, fill a Worksheet out for each of the classrooms and/or teachers you observed. Now compare your results to see if any patterns emerge.

Reflective Narrative

Relate your observations on the classroom characteristics and climate with the goals of democratic participation. Were some classrooms more democratic than others? Did these classrooms exhibit particular characteristics and climates in contrast with those that were more autocratic? Which classrooms seemed more effective in meeting the needs of all the students regardless of their abilities? Which classroom did you prefer? What might that indicate about your preferences as a teacher?

Related Readings

Battistich, V., Solomon, D., & Delucchim, K. (1993). Interaction processes and student outcomes in cooperative learning groups. *Elementary School Journal*, *94*(1), 19–32.

Keefe, J. W. (1987). Learning style theory and practice. Reston, VA: NASSP.

Pierce, C. (1994). Importance of classroom climate for at-risk learners. *Journal of Educational Research*, *88*(1), 37–42.

Vandersijde, P. C., & Tomie, W. (1992). The influence of a teacher training program on student perception of classroom climate. *Journal of Education for Teaching*, *18*(3), 287–295.

Wade, R. C. (1994). Teacher education students' views of class discussion: Implications for fostering critical reflection. *Teaching and Teacher Education*, *10*(2), 231–243.

Classroom Characteristics

Indicate where along this continuum you believe the first classroom to be.

Task Oriented _____|_____|_____ Cooperative

Indicate where along this continuum you believe the second classroom to be.

Task Oriented _____|_____|_____ Cooperative

Circle what you believe to be the primary focus of the first classroom.

Student Centered   **Learning Centered**   **Subject Centered**

Circle what you believe to be the primary focus of the second classroom.

Student Centered   **Learning Centered**   **Subject Centered**

Indicate where you believe the first teacher falls on this continuum.

Emotionally Involved _____|_____|_____ **Emotionally Detatched**

Indicate where you believe the second teacher falls on this continuum.

Emotionally Involved _____|_____|_____ **Emotionally Detatched**

FIG 3.6. Classroom Characteristics and Climate Worksheet (reproduce as needed).

SHADOWING A STUDENT[12]

Background

Many times in teacher training programs we neglect the significant portion of time students are at school but not directly engaged with teachers. What happens in the hallways, on the playground, in the cafeteria, and in those classroom interspaces when the attention of the teacher is directed at other individuals? This exercise is designed to investigate the real life of a student for one day. You are trying to understand the world of schooling as seen through the eyes of one student.

Activity

This exercise will be conducted in three phases: the preparation, the observation, and the follow-up.

Phase One: Preparation.   In this phase you will choose a student to shadow for one school day. This activity, of course, requires you to block out one entire school day. Make sure you are at the school at least 20 min before the arrival of the students, and make sure you have made arrangements for the follow-up interview to be conducted with the student at the end of the observation day. Have someone introduce you to the student so he or she is aware that you will be his or her "shadow" that day. Check your institution's requirements regarding the use of human beings as research subjects. Make sure you follow all the regulations of both your institution and the host school system.

Phase Two: Observation.   In this phase your responsibility is to keep up with the student through the entire school day. Do not follow the student into areas where privacy is a matter of course such as conferences with faculty and/or administrators, the restroom, the infirmary, locker rooms, and the like. Using the observation form from Fig 3.7, record the activities of the student in approximately 5-min intervals. Record the time, the observed behavior(s), and your understandings of what is occurring (e.g., the student seems bored, excited, etc.) For example:

Time	Observed behavior(s)	Interpretation
9:05	Working in teams with computer.	Seems more interested in *partner* than the task at hand!

Phase Three: Follow-up.   This phase is to be conducted with the student at or near the end of the school day, depending on both your schedules. During this time you should ask questions and record his or her responses. Do not be confrontational or argumentative about anything you observed during the day. Your job is to observe, record, and understand the school as seen through the student's eyes—not to judge. You should certainly ask follow-up questions as the student responds to the primary questions, but only for research purposes, not as a form of adjudication or censure.

Reflective Afterthoughts

How does this student understand the school and what is going on? Is this different from what the teachers believe and what you believed from your previous observations? What implications might we draw about how classroom realities are constructed differently by different individuals?

What are the implications for your future work as a teacher?

Related Readings

Ellis, J. (1994). Narrative inquiry with children: A generative form of preservice teacher research. *Qualitative Studies in Education, 7*(4), 75–88.

Jardine, D. W. (1989). There are children all around us. *Journal of Educational Thought, 22*(2), 184–193

Van Manen, M. (1990). *Researching the lived experience: Human sciences for an action sensitive pedagogy*. Ontario, Canada: The University of Western Ontario.

Time	Observed Behavior(s)	Interpretation

FIG. 3.7. Shadowing a Student Data Form (reproduce as needed).

STUDENT RESISTANCE

Background

For years, many researchers and teachers have worked from the assumption that students were simply passive receptors of knowledge. Because of that, any student behavior not within these parameters of passivity was deemed to be "deviant," and the student was dealt with accordingly. We now know that students are not passive but rather active players in the education process. This means that students have choices as to the nature of their participation running from compliance to resistance.

Resistance can take many forms, both active and passive. Openly subverting the teacher's plans, refusing to follow directions, interrupting, and talking out of turn are all examples of active resistance. Passive resistance is much more subtle but just as effective. Failing to answer, letting the attention wander, sleeping, and daydreaming are all examples of passive resistance.

Activity

Dedicate a portion of your observation time to the issue of student resistance. Watch the students who are not behaving within the norms of classroom rules. What are they doing? Be specific. Are these active or passive acts of resistance? Talk to the students to determine why they did what they did. Were they bored? Were

they confused? Were they attempting to hide embarrassment or confusion?

Reflective Narrative

Not all behavioral issues in a classroom are the result of deviance. One challenging question that should arise from this exercise concerns the difficulty of determining which acts are resistance and which are simply behavioral issues. Not all misbehavior or passivity are resistance acts. Conversely, not all misbehavior and passivity are socially deviant. How can you tell the difference? Why is it important to know?

Related Readings

Bullough, R. V., Jr., Gitlin, A. D., & Goldstein, S. L. (1984) Ideology, teacher role, and resistance. *Teachers College Record, 86*(4), 339–358.

Everhardt, R. B. (1983). *Reading, writing, and resistance: Adolescents and labor in a junior high school.* Boston, MA: Routledge & Kegan Paul.

Fine, M. (1986). Why urban adolescents drop into and out of public high school. *Teachers College Record, 87,* 393–410.

Gotfrit, L. (1988). Women dancing back: Disruption and the politics of pleasure. *Journal of Education, 170*(3), 122–141.

Willis, P. (1984). *Learning to labour: How working class kids get working class jobs.* Merrymount, England: Saxon House.

STUDENT RIDICULE AND HARASSMENT

Background

Ever since I can remember, I have been overweight. However, I was used to being teased and had learned to "deal with it." Usually it came from my peers, but this particular day, it came from a different and quite unexpected source. On this particular day, another girl, who was also overweight, had been teased. Everyone except me had called her "jellybelly." And of course she did not like it. She began crying, and I went with her to tell the teacher what had happened. The teacher was very understanding and comforted the girl. As I turned away to go back to the playground, the teacher made a very unexpected comment. She said to me, "Well, Bernice, I don't understand why they didn't pick on you. You are much fatter than she is, and anyone with eyes can see that!" She chuckled, and two of her colleagues who were sitting next to her joined in on the frolic. I was stunned. I just could not believe that a teacher would say something like that to a student. I felt my lip start to quiver, and before I realized it, I blurted out, "You're not so skinny yourself!" With that, she jumped up and took me straight to the principal's office.[13]

As we can witness in the preceding excerpt from the writing of a preservice teacher discussing her significant past school experiences, certain aspects of school life effect some students more than others. Ridicule and harassment are two of these aspects. As we move toward adulthood, this aspect of school life fades in our memory. We have learned how to address more directly most of the confrontational issues that face us in daily life. However, when we were children and adolescents, these strategies were still forming, and the issues of ridicule and harassment loomed large in our daily lives.

Activity

Position yourself in a central location where students congregate between classes or during breaks. This might be a hallway, the cafeteria area, or a playground. Observe the student behaviors and the exchanges that occur. Pay particular attention to comments and actions intended to demean and harass. Note the actions and the individuals or groups at whom these actions are directed.

Reflective Afterthoughts

Who was doing the harassing? Were there patterns to their predations? Who were the targets? How did they react? Did they resist? Did they flee? Can you construct an explanation for these actions? What seemed to be the basis for the intolerance you observed? Was it racial, socioeconomic, gendered, physical, cultural, or something else?

What is your responsibility as a future teacher both legally and ethically to student ridicule and harassment? What did you do? How did this experience make you feel? Did you address any of these issues in the Significant Past School Experiences exercise?

Related Readings

American Association of University Women. (1993). *Hostile hallways: The AAUW survey on sexual harassment in America's schools.* Washington, DC: Author and National Education Association.

Kleinfeld, J. S. (1995). The boys on the bus: Bad language or sexual harassment? In J. S. Kleinfeld

& S. Yerian (Eds.), *Gender tales: Tensions in the schools*, (pp. 149–155). Mahwah, NJ: Lawrence Erlbaum Associates.

Mazer, N. (1993). *Out of control*. New York: Avon Books. (a young adult novel about sexual harassment)

Whatley, M. H. (1988). Raging hormones and powerful cars: The construction of men's sexuality in school sex education and popular adolescent films. *Journal of Education, 170*(3), 100–121.

NOTES

[1]Jackson, P. W. (1968). *Life in classrooms.* Chicago: University of Chicago Press.

[2]Martin, J. R. (1976). What do we do with a hidden curriculum when we find one? *Curriculum Inquiry, 6*(2), 57–74.

[3]Altbach, P. G., Kelly, G. P., Petrie, H. G., & Weis, L. (Eds.). (1991). *Textbooks in American society: Politics, policy, and pedagogy.* Albany: State University of New York Press.

[4]Shannon, P. (1992). Commercial reading materials, a technological ideology, and the deskilling of teachers. In P. Shannon (Ed.), *Becoming political* (pp. 182–207). Portsmouth, NH: Heinemann, p. 196.

[5]Adapted from Page, F. (1994). *Guidelines for student teaching.* Statesboro, GA: Georgia Southern University.

[6]Hart, L. (1983). *Human brain and human learning* (p. 10). New York: Longman.

[7]Laughlin, C. D., McMannus, J., & D'Aquilli, G. G. (1990). *Brain, symbol, & experience: Toward a neurophenomenology of human consciousness.* Boston: New Science Library.

[8]Adapted from an exercise developed by Jane Page, Fred Page, and Donald Hawk (1977), Statesboro, GA: Georgia Southern University.

[9]*Ibid.*

[10]Fischer, B. B., & Fischer, L. (1979). Styles in teaching and learning. *Educational Leadership, 36*(January), 251.

[11]*Ibid.*

[12]Adapted from an exercise developed by Professor Ronnie Shepherd, Department of Middle Grades and Secondary Education, Georgia Southern University, Statesboro Georgia.

[13]Anonymous. (1995). *Reflection paper 1.* Unpublished manuscript (p. 1). Georgia Southern University, Statesboro, Georgia.

Section 4

The School as an Ecosystem

INTRODUCTION

An important activity for beginning teacher educators is to reflect on the notions of elite power and control, and on democratic participation and decision making as they relate to the local, state, and national levels in our educational bureaucracy. Strong differences within the educational community exist about where certain educational decisions should reside and who should participate in their resolution. This issue has become more complex and complicated in recent years as the United States has become part of the larger global community and geopolitical world system.

Some educators, for example, are convinced that a greater centralization of power and a more authoritarian state is absolutely essential if the United States is to solve successfully the massive social, economic, and ecological problems that confront the nation. Others have a different response to the social crises that confront us. These educators are convinced that the increasing centralization of power is a major contributing cause of the crises, not the cure. As such, they believe that the gradual transfer of power, authority, and control of resources away from neighborhoods, towns, and local schools has undermined our ability, willingness, and initiative to participate in the development of more truly creative and authentic community-based solutions to the problems that confront us. As a preservice teacher educator, it is essential that you grapple with some of the specific dimensions of this complex issue as you pursue your own search for more democratic, participatory, and collaborative models of classroom and school leadership.

In conceptualizing an approach to this section, the authors decided that exploring metaphors of schooling would be an interesting way to illuminate some competing assumptions, values, norms, control mechanisms, power relationships, and informal communication networks that underlie the organizational culture of American public schooling. Specifically, the images of the school as a factory or machine and as a living ecological web or community network are employed to help you envision and clarify both the potential dangers and the untapped resources that reside in our ideas about schooling in a democratic society. In this section the authors have sought to develop a series of reflective exercises that will enable you to investigate some of the basic assumptions about your own host school's organizational structures and cultures. This is so that you might examine them critically and perhaps offer some strategies for creating individually liberating and socially empowering school environments. First, we preview the topics of our study.

Metaphoric Images of Schooling

- Metaphors of Classroom Praxis
- Images in the Classroom

Metaphors help shape the way we view the world and enable us to envision more clearly new ways of understanding ourselves, especially during times of rapid social change. The educational literature is rich in metaphors describing the nature and functioning of the American public school system. These metaphors assist us in our efforts to think about, understand, and describe the ambiguities and complexities of school life. Whether helping us conceive of ourselves as part of a larger interconnected ecological web of human existence or merely as parts of a mechanistic machine designed to serve the interests of an elite few, metaphors can profoundly influence the ways that we choose to participate in the educational process.

Metaphors about schooling have, of course, changed along with our evolving perspectives on our relationship to the world around us. A wide variety of metaphors are available in today's educational literature. In everyday educational discourse and literature, schools are frequently pictured as prisons, factories, shopping malls, families, or gardens. Some like to think of schools as ticking clocks or well-oiled machines that never miss a beat. Others conceptualize schools as high-tech space ships designed to launch the participants into the new age of high technology. In many of these metaphors, dramatic contradictions and tensions reflect the competing visions and priorities that different social groups have for the public school system.

Two metaphoric images often used in the analysis of organizational life portray the school as a factory or machine and as a living web or community network. These images enable us to envision ways that actions taken by school organizations affect the habitats, cultures, and ecosystems (for better or worse) in which the schools reside. The image of the community network conveys a vision of each school as a dynamic element in the interconnected web of the local geocultural ecological system. In sharp contrast, a factory carries the impression of a dehumanizing machine that demands conformity, routine, and standardization. Although these metaphoric images are useful for contextualizing oneself in the modern world, and in helping us to understand better the kind of tensions and possibilities within organizational life (particularly that of the U.S. public school system), they tend to represent the ideological opposites of the educational system. Most school organizational structures and cultures rest somewhere between these metaphorical opposites. The preservice teacher can learn, therefore, a great deal about the nature of education and schooling in today's society by exploring these competing metaphoric images.

The metaphor of the factory or machine has become a popular and powerful tool for understanding the nature and functioning of the public

school system. Early in the 20th century Franklin Bobbitt argued that "education is a shaping process as much as the manufacture of steel rails,"[1] and urged his fellow educators to apply the principles of scientific management to every aspect of school administration and operation. In the same way, the sociologist Edward Ross suggested that to educate was "to collect little plastic lumps of human dough from private households and shape them on the social kneading board."[2] School administrators often are compared to factory managers, concerned only with the bottom line: efficiency, productivity, product, work pace, and the like. Perhaps the most important aspect of this metaphor is that it speaks to the technical operational nature of our human relationships and renders all natural aspects of life as largely instrumental: Humans, the environment, animals, industry all are subsumed under the concept of the machine.

This technological vision of organizations was rapidly applied to education. Today, educators argue that schools are formal organizations and, as such, are like giant computers with inputs and outputs, feedback loops, scientifically generated curriculum, and standardized evaluation systems. Administrators are seen as responsible for keeping the gears running smoothly, ensuring the efficient operation of daily work routines and the general maintenance of the school facilities. They are empowered to supervise, punish, evaluate, and reward so as to maintain operational efficiency.

Teachers are forced into a dependency relationship with school administrators and the rest of the educational hierarchy. They work under conditions largely beyond their control, implementing national and state-mandated standards in which they have little or no input. Underlying such top-down mechanistic approaches to educational decision making are unstated beliefs about the desirability of having large-scale federal- and state-level educational bureaucracies set nationwide standardized systems of evaluation. Robert Heilbroner, for example, argued, "I not only predict but I prescribe a centralization of power as the only means by which our threatened and dangerous civilization can make way for its successor."[3]

The image of the school as an ecological web is grounded in the image of caring, sharing, and mutual coexistence. Because we all are connected, we all should act cooperatively to maintain and preserve our collective work environments. Perhaps de Chardin expressed it best when he wrote:

> The farther and more deeply we penetrate into matter, by means of increasingly powerful methods, the more we are confounded by the interdependence of its parts. Each element of the cosmos is positively woven from all the others. … It is impossible to cut into this network, to isolate a portion without it becoming frayed and unraveled at all its edges. All around us, as far as the eye can see, the universe holds together, and only one way of considering it is really possible, that is, to take it as a whole, in one piece.[4]

From this perspective, one's living body is seen as part of a complex but fragile system of interdependent relationships that depends on cooperation, connectedness, and community for its very existence. Here, we see ourselves and others as part of a collective whole, an organic "Gaia," a universal classroom, a part of an interconnected global web of alliances and obligations. At its core, then, the living body web metaphor resonates with a concern for the delicacy of the strands that connect us and provide us with sustenance: It dramatically captures the theme that we affect everything and everything affects us.

This metaphor of the school as a living body or community web is one that we often use more commonly in rhetorical writings about education. In such formulations, the school often is described as a family, home, team, or womb. The principal is described as a parent, nurturer, friend, sibling, or coach. In such school organizational cultures, colleagues have a great concern for one another as well as a commitment to students that goes above and beyond the call of duty. Not unlike that of biological families, an extensive network exists of informal food, entertainment, sports, and holiday rituals (i.e., birthday celebrations, betting pools, informal communication networks, friendly jokes, etc.)

that binds the faculty and staff to one another and provides multiple avenues for socializing and bonding. In such schools, teachers view each other as competent professionals who may not always agree with one another but who must respect one another and have each other's best interest in heart. Parents are welcomed guests and volunteers. Teachers and students share tasks and co-negotiate learning options in education cultures that are collegial, respectful, and collaborative. Participants accept the legitimacy and authority of the organization because they are an integral part of the decision-making process.

These metaphoric oppositions can be more closely examined to illustrate both the pitfalls and possibilities that exist in our educational settings today. They also have the ability to help us understand some of our own changing attitudes toward education and analyze some of the existing tensions in public school environments. We invite you to do just this in the exercise developed for this section.

Studying About Your Host School's Power Structures

- Student Governance
- Faculty and Staff Governance
- The Role of the Local School Board
- The Process of Educational Decision Making

Contemporary school reform literature is replete with metaphors, images, and words that convey democratic principles and values. Central to any contemporary discourse or textual elaboration of the current school reform initiatives are words such as community, community control, decentralization, participation, empowerment, parental involvement, student decision making, teacher control, local control, site-based management, the self-managed school, collaborative decision making, self-determining school systems, and parental choice. These words lead one to believe that educational structures and processes have indeed begun to move toward more locally based and participatory democratic forms. Is it true that the metaphor of the school as a factory has begun to be replaced by that of the school as an ecological web?

Many educational theorists and school practitioners point out, however, that the hoped-for shift in the nature of educational decision making from the older models of control-oriented, top-down management to more democratic modes of local site-based management has not occurred.[5] These same educational theorists have begun to point out that the national educational "empowerment" discourse of the 1990s only functions to obscure and mask the recentralization of educational decision making in a professional elite that actually is occurring throughout the educational bureaucracy. Smyth asked some troubling questions concerning the precise nature of this latest school reform strategy:

> The paradox is that at precisely the same time we are experiencing a hardening of the educational arteries through moves to make schooling more "rigorous," "disciplined," and "scholarly" (all of which are only really possible in circumstances where final decision-making is vested in the hands of an elite decision-making group), we are also being courted by moves that appear to make the schools more "self-determining" and "self-renewing," with teachers who are more "autonomous," "empowered," "collaborative," and "reflective." How do we explain this paradox?[6]

This second group of exercises has been developed to help you think about some of the issues involved in this current educational debate within the context of your own host school. What has been the impact of the latest school restructuring efforts at your school? We invite you to look beyond the rhetoric of the school reform literature today and study the actual changes that have been institutionalized as part of the current school restructuring movement at your school. Ask your colleagues: Have the new models of site-based management been more emancipatory and liberating for teachers, students, and school administrators? Or has the current school restructuring movement functioned only to allow a system of national standards, curriculum, evaluation, and testing to be adopted within a framework that puts the burden of implementation, funding, and accountability on local school systems? Is this real

democratic decision making? As future educators, it is essential that you develop the kind of critical consciousness and analytic skills that will allow you to investigate these issues in greater depth. These exercises are also designed to encourage you to think about what a more socially, culturally, and politically empowering approach to democratic decision making might resemble.

Exploring School–Community Linkages

- Assessing Family–School Relationships
- Assessing the Parent–Teacher Relationship
- School-to-Work Linkages
- Extracurricular School Activities
- Rebellion, Conformity, and Making Do
- Violent Schools–Safe Schools: Police–Military Linkages
- Consumerism in the Classroom
- Cyberspace and the Virtual Classroom

We hear a lot these days about a "sense of community." More and more of us, we're told, are seeking it. We talk about the African-American, Hispanic, and Asian communities; the gay and lesbian community; the New Age community; the political community; the university community; a community of peers; a community of interests; the local community. But what is this thing called community? Why do we seek it? How do we know when we find it?[7]

What is a democratic community? What are the purposes of public schools? Indeed, the very concepts of *community* and *democracy* have become obscure and somewhat remote from our everyday lived experiences. We often hear others say that democratic forms of self-government have become increasingly irrelevant in today's high-tech global economy, and that we need to generate more realistic, professionally viable, and managed forms of democratic participation. It is clear that we live in an age with multiple perspectives on what constitutes a democratic community and democratic schooling. Some argue that schools should be an arena in which special interest groups are allowed to compete within the framework of a free market ideology based on self-interest, competition, and choice.[8] McDaniel[9] and Shea[10] argued that much of this school reform rhetoric is grounded in military metaphors and images such as strategic planning, systems analysis, social efficiency, accountability, and disciplinary enforcement. The power of such metaphoric images of schooling is in their ability to define what and who shall be included or excluded from the discussion, decision making, and implementation of educational policy.

By contrast, educators such as Kozol[11], Orr[12], Bowers[13], Smith[14], Traina and Darley-Hill,[15] among others, have emphasized that the revival of more democratic, participatory forms of public schooling in the United States rests on the simultaneous rebuilding of local communities, small towns, urban wards, and cohesive neighborhood networks that have suffered from decades of neglect. *Bioregionalism* is the name given to these various attempts to rejuvenate regional and local institutions in order to recreate the kind of rich system of interactive and participatory local networks needed for healthy community-based schools in the 21st century. Along similar lines, others have argued that the top-down, control-oriented models of democratic management have resulted in the decline of local communities as repositories of commitment, loyalty, and obligation. Only by a revival of such soulful and intimate community structures can authentic local traditions and values flourish and be reinforced, developed, and celebrated. Winters reminded us that "community should be a place where compassion abounds and where individuals are valued for their uniqueness."[16]

We wonder anew: Who should control our schools and how? In the United States, with our multilayered governmental bureaucratic structures, educational decision making is formally distributed and delegated among a variety of professional groups, including state and federal judges, the Secretary of Education, appointed Presidential advisors, the Congress and state legislatures, mayors and city councils, and civil servant bureaucrats. In addition, a variety of extralegal pressure groups vie for power and control at the federal, state, and local levels of the educational bureaucracy. Such groups include professional groups, teacher unions, philanthropic foundations, corporate leaders, organized special interest groups, think tanks, and lobbyists. The plethora of competing and allied groups makes it imperative that we describe and differentiate between competing models of democratic empowerment and control.[17]

Although drawing analogies between school organizations and factories, and picturing school organizations as interconnected community webs helps us reflect on some characteristics that define different organizational structures, it does not allow us to experience the innermost essence of school cultures: those taken-for-granted, invisible, and often unconscious aspects of school life. Recent educational writings have identified a number of these elements through which school organizational structures and cultures are preserved, expressed, and conveyed, including the history of the school, symbolic myths and stories, values and beliefs, behavioral norms, rites and rituals, and heroes and heroines. These cultural forms and the hidden network of informal connections and relationships will also be a part of your observations and reflections in this section.

Your exploration of these competing metaphors of schooling will illuminate some opposing assumptions, values, norms, control mechanisms, power relationships, and informal communication networks that underlie the organizational cultures in our public schools. The aim of these exercises is not to force you to choose one metaphor over another, but rather to show you the ways in which our public schools have become complex, political arenas in which differing social groups seek to realize their individual educational agendas. In the end, you will return, as you began, with the question: What is the nature of a democratic community? What are (and should be) the purposes of democratic schools? How can I as a politically informed teacher work toward further democratizing our public school classrooms?

METAPHORS OF CLASSROOM PRAXIS

Background

Metaphor plays an important part in human thought processes. Although commonly associated with poetry, metaphors increase our understanding in many fields, enabling us to understand one kind of thing in terms of another. In this way, we gain a greater understanding of an unfamiliar or complex object or idea in terms of a more familiar or less complex object or idea. Additionally, metaphors provide a bridge of understanding by establishing a common connection between two people experiencing difficulty grasping one another's perspectives.

For example, a common metaphor useful for the fieldwork experience portrays the classroom as a mirror of the larger society. Our familiarity with the relatively simple mirror concept can be used to enhance our understanding of the more complex concept of public schools. Through exploring this metaphor, we can reflect on educational issues from a new perspective and generate new insights on possible connections between school structures and classroom praxis.[18]

Activity

In the following list are metaphors commonly used in describing the American public school system today: Education as

war
drugstore
factory
prison
shopping mall
stream
family
journey
garden
smorgasbord
spaceship
living body
circus
cemetery
ant colony

Select one metaphor from the preceding list or create one of your own for further exploration. Consider first the classroom environment that you are observing. How is the metaphor you selected represented? You may want to start by making a list of terms from education that correspond to the metaphor you have selected. For example, if you selected "war," who is the enemy? What are the weapons? Who is the supply sergeant, the general, the deserters, the casualties? How do classroom materials relate to the metaphor?

Write a brief analysis of your insights. What is the significance of the observations you made? What can you determine about the extent to which this metaphor represents an ideal to which we can aspire or a danger that we should attempt to avoid?

Consider also the implications of this metaphor for teachers, students, administrators, and parents. What kind of teacher–student relationships does the metaphor encourage? What role does the metaphor suggest for parents? What does this metaphor indicate about the curriculum? Are certain subjects highlighted by the use of this metaphor? Are other subjects difficult to imagine within this context?

Reflective Narrative

You may want to select a second metaphor to explore for comparison or to compare with those chosen by your classmates. How does this second metaphor change the way you think about schools? Can you think of other metaphors that may relate to education? How do these other perspectives affect your understanding of the activities of schooling? Does any single metaphor account for every aspect and dimension of education? What metaphor do you think is best and why? In what ways might these metaphors influence our experiences (and behaviors) in schools?

Related Readings

Davidson, D. (1978). What metaphors mean. *Critical Inquiry, (5)*, 31–47.

Giroux, H. A. (1981). *Ideology, culture, and the process of schooling.* London: Falmer Press.

Lakoff, G., & Johnson, M. (1980). *Metaphors we live by.* Chicago: University of Chicago Press (See especially Concepts We Live By [pp. 3–6] and Metaphor and Cultural Coherence [pp. 22–24]).

Morgan, G. (1986). *Images of organization.* Beverly Hills, CA: Sage.

Rehm, M. (1994). Critical pedagogy and vocational education: A search for new metaphors. In R. D. Lakes (Ed.), *Critical education and work: Multidisciplinary approaches* (pp. 143–160). Norwood, NJ: Ablex.

IMAGES IN THE CLASSROOM

Background

We are constantly surrounded by images of all kinds. One frequently overlooked aspect of the classroom environment is the images. In today's schools, almost every classroom has a television set and computers that relay images to students and teachers. But other images are in the classroom: bulletin boards with photographs, illustrations, drawings, and announcements. Although we often tune out these images, they still affect our behaviors and attitudes and reveal much about the values embedded in the daily practice of schooling.

Activity

Take inventory of the images you see in the classroom. What is being represented? Are films, videos, or television programs part of the curriculum? What commercials or advertisements are associated with these programs?

What about the bulletin boards in the classroom? Are these announcement centers, or decorations? Are they used in conjunction with the curriculum materials and texts? Do they support formal learning? Are the images stale or are they replaced frequently?

Notice also the images in the textbooks. How is the artwork presented in the texts, on the covers? What images are found within the texts? Who is represented? What are they doing? Note differences in gender, race or ethnicity, and social class. How are various social groups depicted? After making a thorough accounting of the images in the classroom, gather your data and write up your analysis.

Reflective Narrative

Do the images in the classroom present a coherent and carefully planned message? Are they consistent and complementary in their presentations, or are they contradictory and confusing? How are the images in the classroom different from images in religious settings, shopping malls, homes, restaurants, and highways?

What kinds of images did you still overlook in your first observation? Did you find images on notebooks, pens, and pencils? Did you note clothes of students and teacher that advertise products or ideas? Did you find any desks, chairs, or other objects in the room with images carved on them? Make another inspection of the room, and determine what you may have left out the first time. Why were these images overlooked during your first inspection?

Related Readings

Douglas, S. (1994). *Where the girls are: Growing up female with the mass media.* New York: Times Books.

Ellsworth, E., & Whatley, M. H. (Eds.). (1990). *The ideology of images in educational media: Hidden curriculums in the classroom.* New York: Teachers College Press.

McLaren, P. (1986). *Schooling as ritual performance: Towards a political economy of educational symbols and gestures.* London: Routledge & Kegan Paul.

Spring, J. (1994). *Images of American life: A history of ideological management in schools, movies, radio, and television.* Albany: State University of New York Press.

98

Videorecordings:

Riggs, M. J. (1987). *Ethnic notions*. San Francisco: California News Reel.

Kilbourn, J. (1987). *Still killing us softly: Advertising images of women*. Cambridge, MA: Cambridge Documentary films.

STUDENT GOVERNANCE AND DECISION MAKING

Background

Student governance and decision making are perhaps the most controversial and least understood components in the new site-based management models of school restructuring. Students are not generally viewed as having the cognitive, psychological, moral, or emotional maturity needed to make reasonable and responsible choices concerning their own educational programs, learning environments, and work pace. Students usually are viewed as consumers or products of the educational process; teachers are viewed as the proper classroom authorities in all matters related to curriculum, pedagogy, rules, and discipline. Most school curricula are set, and instruction is centered on the mastery of a state-mandated set of grade-specific standards. Nationally standardized tests control and shape an increasing amount of the students' in-class learning experiences and required texts. Not unexpectedly, this sort of top-down classroom "colonization" of students has resulted in myriad forms of student subservience, acquiescence, passivity, retreat, disruption, and revolt.[19]

As school systems struggle to revise and transform older administrative structures based on top-down management systems designed to ensure compliance, order, predictability, and social control, new concepts of school leadership and empowerment have been adopted by school administrators, teachers, and students. The school in which you presently reside most likely contains an odd combination of both organizational models. Student empowerment suggests that students are a central part of the educational process and should be encouraged to take increasing responsibility for their educational work. In this sense, teachers and students share tasks and co-negotiate learning options in educational cultures that are collegial, respectful, and collaborative. The goal of student empowerment is to take a student from dependency to independence.[20]

Activity

This exercise is designed to position you as an investigator into the nature and degree of student power and participation in the decision-making structures of the larger school organization.

1. Obtain and examine a copy of the student handbook at your host school. What topics are addressed? What do most of the standing regulations seem to address: behavior? clothing? conformity? allegiance to the organization?[21]

2. Attend some of the regularly scheduled meetings of the student government. Discover how student government is organized at your school and what specific responsibilities are delegated to it? What is the scope and nature of the decision-making powers assigned to the student government? Do most of the "decisions" appear to be preordained? What issues appear to be out of bounds? For example, to what extent is student government involved in course selection and development, teacher evaluation, school management and budget decisions, scheduling decisions, luncheon menus, and disciplinary procedures? Is student government largely relegated to decisions concerning bulletin boards, prom queen, fund raisers, weekend dance or events arrangements, or class trip planning? Do you feel

a sense of real empowerment in this group? If so, why? To what do you attribute this?

Reflective Narrative

Most student organizations have very limited powers and regularly address only issues of little relevance to the larger school and district-wide educational bureaucracies. Interview some of the student leaders and members of the various student cliques concerning their perceptions of the school power structures. Through informal conversations with these various student subcultures, attempt to develop a slang classificatory system for all terms used to identify student groups in the school (i.e., the nerds, the jocks, the social climbers, the preppies, the druggies, etc.). Ask them some of the following questions: Who seems to control the dominant culture of the student organizations in terms of defining the acceptable boundaries of behavior? Which student subgroups are most actively involved in

student government and why? How is membership determined? Do the student leaders seem to represent all the students or just a particular subculture of the students? Or are they merely those most willing to implement mandates from the administrative staff?

Related Readings

Apple, M., & Beane, J. A. (1995). *Democratic schools*. Alexandria, VA: Association for Supervision and Curriculum Development.

Eckert, P. (1989). *Jocks and burnouts: Social categories and identity in the high school*. New York: Teachers College Press.

Greenberg, D. (1991). *Free at last: The Sudbury Valley School*. Framingham, MA: Sudbury Valley School Press.

Smith, G. A. (1993). *Public schools that work*. New York: Routledge & Kegan Paul.

Wood, G. (1992). *Schools that work*. New York: Dutton.

FACULTY AND STAFF GOVERNANCE

Background

Schools are both organizations and communities. They contain within them sophisticated networks (formal and informal) of adult subcultures (e.g., the administrators, teachers, coaches, maintenance staff, secretaries, paraprofessionals, tenured and nontenured faculty, males and females, etc.) as well as youth subcultures. Although each of these subcultures has its own informal boundaries, rituals, and rules, they all must exist and function within the boundaries and regulations of the larger school organizational structure, interacting with one another and the larger society. This larger school culture is considered the dominant culture, whereas the others are regarded as subcultures. School rules and regulations are often ways of maintaining the dominant culture of the organization against the dynamic pressures from subcultural groups for greater participation. School rules also work to maintain a certain set of power relationships between various groups in the school. The manner in which governance (decision making) occurs within the organization is clearly linked to these interests of power.[21]

Subcultural groups both control and are controlled by the school organizations in which they serve. In a sense, there is a continual dialogue among subcultural groups themselves and with the administrative elite. This creates a dynamic tension in a school no matter how autocratic, conformist, or participatory its basic organizational structure. In most American public schools, these subcultural relationships are perceived as threats to the status quo and impediments to the smooth top-down administration of the educational bureaucracy. Thus, a dominant organizational culture develops dedicated largely to managing change and maintaining control.[22]

Activity

Examine the manner in which faculty governance is conducted at your host school.[23] How is governance organized? What is its position on a flow chart of the school or the school district? Who serves? How is membership determined? Are the faculty "leaders" chosen merely to be rubber stamps of administrative decisions, or is it the other way around with administrators selected because they have a history of supporting teacher empowerment? Who are the department or program chairpersons? What are their roles and responsibilities? Does any one person or any one group have the informal power to control decision making? How did they gain such informal power and influence?

What issues are addressed by these faculty and staff groups? How much real input does the faculty have regarding curricular, personnel, programs, policy, or financial decisions? Is faculty governance merely advisory or does the faculty have any real power of decision making? Observe how and what changes take place at your host school. Do the faculty seem most concerned with meeting their own needs, satisfying administrators, or helping students?

Do the faculty at the school appear to be satisfied or concerned about the decision-making power they have (or do not have) at this school? If they are concerned about their lack of empowerment, does it get expressed through the formal political process or more often through informal acts of defiance and resistance (i.e., leaving when the school bell rings, sitting passively in faculty meetings, etc.)? Are the custodial staff, secretaries, and paraprofessionals ever included in the faculty decision-making bodies? If not, why?

In what kind of political activity are the faculty at your host school allowed to participate (Are they allowed to become actively involved in school board elections or hold political office? Are teachers allowed to organize at the school? Have there been any strikes? If so, what were the issues? Talk to the teachers, particularly the union organizers. Do the teachers' organizations influence decision making at the school? How much influence do they exert? What are the issues? Are there union contracts at the school? Review these contracts for their provisions regarding salaries, curriculum structuring, class size, and so forth. Do you see any connections being established between teacher governance structures, increased democratic decision-making formats, and greater community involvement in the school?

Reflective Narrative

How do the faculty and staff governance structures compare with the student governance structures? Whose interests do the faculty governance structures seem to favor: staffs'? teachers'? administrators'? parents'? no one's? Are the administrative, faculty, staff, and student governance structures mutually informing and supportive, or do their aims seem to be at odds with one another?

Related Readings

Ayers, W. (1993). *To teach: The journey of a teacher.* New York: Teachers College Press.

Carlson, D. (1992). *Teachers and crisis: Urban school reform and teachers' work culture.* New York: Routledge & Kegan Paul.

Miller, J. P. (1993). *The holistic teacher.* Toronto: Ontario Institute for Studies in Education.

Shor, I. (1992). *Empowering education: Critical teaching for social change.* Chicago: University of Chicago Press.

Smyth, J. (1991). *Teachers as collaborative learners: Challenging dominant forms of supervision.* Philadelphia: Open University Press.

THE ROLE OF LOCAL SCHOOL BOARDS

Background

The framers of the United States Constitution made no mention of education, but left that responsibility, instead, to the states through the reserved powers' clause. In turn, most states, in their constitution or laws, decided that the operational governance functions for schools should reside in local school boards. In the 19th century, governance was lodged in school boards largely responsive to local community cultures and traditions. However, by the 1890s, rapid immigration, urbanization, industrialization, and business consolidations brought many changes to American society. As part of the progressive municipal reform movement, educational governance systems were centralized, and 120,000 local school boards were consolidated into what is now only about 15,000. Leadership shifted to a new professional middle-class group trained in the theories of scientific management, and large statewide educational bureaucracies grew at exponential rates. Today, almost one half of our public school population is enrolled in only 1% of our school districts. As a result, many concede that we have now constructed massive educational bureaucracies that enable national and state control over almost every aspect of local schooling in the United States.[24]

The Institute for Educational Leadership[25] issued a major report on school boards in 1986. The report concluded that school boards lacked both the capacity for meaningful goal setting and the ability to make plans to accomplish specific local goals. School boards, it seems, were not willing to take the political risks needed to provide leadership for locally generated school re-

forms. School board members were not taking the time really to learn about the issues and seemed reluctant to decentralize decision making to school sites. Board members appeared to be more comfortable with national and state centralized systems of control over local school districts, especially regarding reform efforts to implement national standards, curricula, and standardized testing.

Local school boards are being lobbied by teacher unions, parent groups, and local business coalitions to provide a greater degree of local power, control, and decision making concerning local school governance structures, curricula content, and overall school programs and policies. Thus, the local school board has once again become an arena for political struggles between those seeking greater national and state control over local schools and those advocating increased democratic participation and decision making by the local community, parents, and teachers. Your own local school board also likely reflects many of these same tensions and struggles.

Activity

Attend a local school-board meeting. Before or after the meeting introduce yourself to some members of the school board and ask whether you might interview them either in person or by phone at a time and place convenient for them.

After gathering some initial profile data on your school-board member, tell your interviewee that you would like to find out more about what school-related issues are of most interest to school-board members. Use the chart from Fig 4.1 to record the board member's responses.

Reflective Narrative

Study the responses made by school board members to your survey. Then give the same survey to some of the teachers and administrators at your host school. Do you notice any trends in their responses, especially to your questions about the importance of certain educational issues? Write a short response to your survey indicating how and why your own responses seem to be different from or the same as those provided by school board members, administrators, or the teachers at your host school.

Consider further the following questions: Has the trend toward centralized decision making and standard rules served American education well, considering the purposes of public education you deem legitimate? What have been the positive and negative achievements?

What specific kinds of decision making would you decentralize and destandardize? What might be the positivie benefits, and what problems might you anticipate?

Related Readings

Gittell, M. (1972). *Local control in education*. New York: Praeger.

Grady, M. L. (1995). Superintendents' and school board members' perceptions of empowerment. In M. Richardson, K. Lane, & J. Flanigan (Eds.), *School Empowerment* (pp. 199–212). Lancaster, PA: Technomic Publishing Company.

Institute for Educational Leadership. (1986). *School boards: Strengthening grass roots leadership*. Washington, DC: Author.

Spring, J. (1996). *American education* (7th ed.), (pp. 171–192). New York: McGraw-Hill.

School-Related Concern	Little Interest	Some Interest	Great Interest
1. Financial support for schools			
2. Collective bargaining for teachers			
3. Parental participation in schools			
4. Site-based management			
5. Finding excellent teachers			
6. School security issues			
7. Inadequate facilities/Computers			
8. Curriculum development issues			
9. School tracking systems			
10. Crime/vandalism/violence			
11. State-mandated curriculum			
12. Racial/ethnic tensions			
13. Education for at-risk students			
14. Student truancy/apathy			
15. School management/leadership			
16. School/Business partnerships			
17. Charter school development			
18. School choice/Vouchers			
19. Implementing national standards			
20. Student diversity/equity issues			

FIG 4.1. School Board Members' Concerns and Interests Survey Form[26] (reproduce as needed).

THE POLITICS OF EDUCATIONAL DECISION MAKING

Background

Before the 1960s, local community participation in educational decision making during the 20th century was limited not only in terms of who participated and how, but also in the range of educational issues deemed appropriate for grassroots input.[27] There was a tacit assumption that most educational decisions required technical expertise, and therefore should be delegated to educational professionals. Issues relating to governance, budget, personnel, curriculum, and discipline were generally considered outside the realm of local citizenry.

Much of this changed as a result of the community control movement in the 1960s as the old consensus broke down. Newly politicized groups of minorities and women, formerly excluded from the educational decision-making process, demanded to be heard. The idea that schools were essentially technocratically engineered, bureaucratic "machines" best run by the professionals was attacked. Although this community control movement did not produce any dramatic restructuring of political power in the educational bureaucracy, it did broaden the scope of local participation in many aspects of school decision making.

At this time, many large city school districts adopted some form of administrative decentralization with varying degrees of community participation. Some school districts began experimental community-controlled schools, and thousands of others added new parent/citizen advisory committees. A number of Indian tribes initiated community control experiments in both public and Bureau of Indian Affairs'

schools near reservations. Generally, it can be concluded that more parents and other nonprofessional community members are participating than ever before in a wide-ranging number and variety of school programs and operations as tutors, volunteers, librarians, lunchroom assistants, hall monitors, classroom paraprofessionals, leaders to extracurricular activities, special resource teachers, and the like.[28]

We are now being inundated with a bewildering array of terms such as school-based management, site-based management, the self-managing school, the self-renewing school, and school empowerment. These terms lead us to conclude that the impact of the current reform movements has been to increase local participation by students, parents, teachers, administrators, and local citizens in all aspects of the local community.

Unmasking appearances is the purpose of the following exercise. Ask yourself the following questions about the nature of educational decision making? In what issues do students, parents, teachers, administrators, and/or local citizens participate? In what ways do they participate? What are the consequences of their participation?

Activity

Complete the left side of the chart from Fig. 4.2 by finding out who actually does control the decision making regarding each of the educational issues listed (list as many numbers as apply).

Complete the right side of this same chart. Interview several teachers and administrators at your school about who should control (or have more input into the decision-making process regarding) each of the educational issues listed. To assist your interviewees, ask them to examine the chart from Fig. 4.3 and tell you who should have more control over each educational issue. Make a list of as many of the numbers as the respondent wishes to use.

Following your survey of teachers and administrators, look around your own classroom and the school classrooms, halls, and meeting rooms. Do you see any explicit messages to the students encouraging their participation in the school decision-making bodies? Are there bulletin boards with up-to-date information on the issues being discussed by students, teachers, administrators, parents, and the local school board? Does the bulletin board provide a listing of the current names, addresses, phone numbers, and e-mail addresses of contact persons within each organization? Are there any formal structures, procedures, or networks so that students can easily provide their informal input on these issues? What recommendations might you make to the school administrators on ways to improve the process by which students can be informed and can contribute their ideas to the various decision-making groups in the school?

Reflective Narrative

Study the responses to your survey made by the teachers and administrators. Did you notice any trends in their responses? For example, did you find that teachers are almost never formally included in most of the important school-related decision making? Did you find that the teachers desired some form of input on most of these issues? Can you think of some good reasons why the insights, perspectives, and experiences of the classroom teachers might be essential in making good policy decisions on these issues? Can you think of reasons why teachers have been excluded from the political process for so long? Did you find that the teachers desired a greater degree of student input on these issues too? If not, why do you think this is the case? Do you think that students should be included to a greater degree in the formal decision-making bodies of the school?

Related Readings

Giroux, H. (1989). Educational reform and teacher empowerment. In H. Holtz, I. Mareus, J. Dougherty, J. Michaels, & R. Peduzzi (Eds.), *Education and the American dream: Conservatives, liberals, and radicals debate the future of education*. Granby, MA: Bergin & Garvey.

Shea, C., Kahane, E., & Sola, P. (Eds.). (1989). *The new servants of power: A critique of the 1980s school reform movement*. New York: Praeger.

Simon, R. I. (1989). Empowerment as a pedagogy of possibility. In H. Holtz, I. Mareus, J. Dougherty, J. Michaels, & R. Peduzzi (Eds.), *Education and the American dream: Conservatives, liberals, and radicals debate the future of education*. Granby, MA: Bergin & Garvey.

Smith, G. (1994). Preparing teachers to restructure schools. *Journal of Teacher Education, 45,* 18–30.

Zeichner, K. (1991). Contradictions and tensions in the professionalism of teaching. *Teachers College Record, 92,* 363–373.

Does Control?	Control What?	Should Control?
	To evaluate student performance?	
	To elect the school principal?	
	To elect a local superintendent?	
	To close a school?	
	Formulate school disciplinary procedures?	
	School schedule?/Classroom schedules?	
	Decide lunchroom menus?	
	Formulate teacher qualification policies?	
	Vote on teacher placement/retention?	
	Choose classroom textbooks?	
	Determine attendance policy?	
	Responsibility for school fiscal policy?	
	Determine school dress policy?	
	Determine classroom-level grading policies?	
	Determine whether school is providing equality of educational opportunity?	
	Number/type of courses for graduation?	
	Mainstreaming policies?	
	Corporal punishment rules?	
	Racial balance of students?	
	Classroom curriculum, textbooks, and methods?	

FIG 4.2. The politics of educational decision making: Who does or should control? (reproduce as needed).

Local Level Groups	State Level Groups
1. Parents at local level	27. State legislatures
2. Local boards of education	28. State boards of education
3. School principal	29. State superintendent
4. Student council	30. The governor
5. Local education associations (PTA)	31. Governor's select committee
6. Teacher council at each school	32. State department of education
7. Teachers	33. Urban city majors
8. Local district superintendent	34. Urban city councils
9. Members/citizens of the community	
10. Students	
11. School staff (e.g., bus drivers, dieticians, health officers, attendance officers)	
12. Local police departments	
13. Local business groups	

National Level Groups	Extralegal/Pressure Groups
14. U.S. President	35. Education experts
15. U.S. Congress	36. Teachers' unions
16. U.S. Supreme Court	37. Textbook companies
17. U.S. Federal government	38. National testing companies (CEEB, ETS)
18. Department of Education	39. Colleges of education
19. Council of Chief State Officers	40. National teachers' unions (AFT and NEA)
20. National teachers' professional organizations	41. Political action coalitions (PACs)
21. Ad hoc national educational task forces convened by U.S. President	42. Ad hoc single issue interest/lobby groups
22. National professional education accreditation/certification boards	43. Private philanthropic foundations (e.g., Carnegie, Rockefeller, MacArthur, etc.)
23. National education standards boards	44. Corporate business leaders (CEOs)
24. Federal district judges	45. Think tank groups (Brookings, Heritage)
25. Secretary of Education	46. Political parties
26. Presidential advisors	47. Lobbyists
	48. Religious organizations and groups

FIG 4.3. Who does or should control? Groups involved in educational decision making (reproduce as needed).

ASSESSING FAMILY–SCHOOL RELATIONSHIPS

Background

An examination of the history of schooling in America provides clear evidence that the separation of the home from the school has a long tradition in public education, dating back to the early Republic period in American history. Horace Mann, for example, thought that poor Irish immigrant parents lacked the moral values, work habits, and social attitudes needed to enculturate their children into the American way of life and industrial work force. Thus, schools were seen as superior and ideal substitutes for the perceived culturally deficient immigrant family culture.[29]

Recent research studies, however, have overwhelmingly demonstrated that where school programs have a strong component of parental involvement, students are consistently better achievers than in identical programs with less parental involvement.[30] Students in schools that maintain frequent contact with parents consistently outperform other schools. These positive effects persist, too, well beyond the short term. For example, children of color and those from low-income families who participated in preschool programs with high levels of parent involvement were still outperforming their peers when they reached senior high school.[31]

Although teachers and school administrators often publicly support the importance of greater parental involvement in the schools in official school communiques, the actual performance of American schools in this regard is less impressive. The term *parental involvement*, too, has been subject to a wide variety of interpretations. Does parental involvement mean that parents should be considered expert advisors? willing volun-

teers? teacher assistants? silent partners? supportive audience? collaborative decision makers? or enthusiastic day-to-day problem solvers? In the following exercise, you are asked to consider ways that educators can nurture and strengthen the family–school relationship.

Activity

Phase One. The checklist developed by the staff at the National Committee for Citizens in Education lists some of these new parental involvement initiatives and provides a diagnostic questionnaire that you can use to evaluate how well your host school is working with parents.[32]

Assessing the Family–School Relationship Checklist (Answer "yes" or "no")

Principle 1: School Climate

_____ Do office personnel greet parents (in person or on the phone) in a friendly, courteous way?

_____ Do posted signs warmly welcome parents and visitors?

_____ Are directions written or posted to help parents and visitors find their way around the school?

_____ Is there a comfortable reception area for parents and visitors, equipped with a coat rack and information about the school?

_____ Is there an orientation program for the incoming class of students and their families?

_____ Is there a program for helping mid-year transfer students and their families to settle into the school (e.g., is a staff member assigned to be their host)?

_____ Are there regular social occasions or events at which parents and school staff can get to know each other?

_____ Does the principal have clearly posted office hours when the parents and students can drop in to talk?

_____ Does the school permit parents to observe in class?

_____ Does the school have an "open door" policy, that welcomes parents at any time during the school day?

_____ Other?

Principle 2: Communication

_____ Is there a school newsletter with up-to-date information about holidays, special events, and the like.

_____ Does the school send home a calendar listing dates of parent–teacher conferences, report cards, holiday schedules, and major events?

_____ Does the school send home a directory of key PTA representatives and school personnel, with phone numbers?

_____ Does the school hold annual back-to-school nights and open houses?

_____ Does the school have a hotline for parents and students to deal with emergencies, rumors, and other burning questions?

_____ Do your policies encourage all teachers to communicate frequently with parents about their curriculum plans, expectations for homework, grading policies, and how they should help?

_____ Do parents know where to go with their concerns, questions, and complaints?

_____ Does the principal review all the school's written communications, including report-card format and how test results are reported, to make sure they are respectful of a parent's adult status and yet easy to understand?

_____ Are parents informed of their rights? This includes access to school records, due process in disciplinary actions, and participation in special education decisions.

_____ Other?

Principle 3: Parents as Collaborators and Problem Solvers

_____ Does the school require at least one parent–teacher conference each year for each student?

_____ Does the school offer to set up teacher–parent conferences on request?

_____ Does the school provide in-service training or other opportunities to help teachers communicate and collaborate with parents?

_____ Is there an early warning policy directing teachers to consult with parents promptly if a child is falling behind or having social behavioral problems?

_____ Does the school inform parents right away if a student does not show up for school? Are parents promptly consulted if there is a pattern of unexcused absences?

_____ Does the elementary school confer with parents on the choice of classroom settings or teacher?

_____ Does the high school require parent approval of a student's choice of courses?

_____ Are training and resources (such as a parent advocate) provided for parents of special-education students to help them participate in the Individualized Education Plan and other processes?

_____ Other?

Principle 4: Parents as Advisors and Decision Makers

_____ Does the school publish and keep current a policy handbook for parents and students that covers discipline, absences, homework, dress standards, parent and student rights, and so forth?)

_____ If the school needs to develop a new policy or program, is there a mechanism for obtaining parent input?

_____ Is there a parent–teacher organization that meets at least once a month?

_____ Do parents ever approach the principal on their own initiative to question school policy or procedures, aside from procedures that affect only their child?

_____ When a problem arises at the school, such as a sharp increase in vandalism or drug use or a significant decline in test scores, does the staff inform and enlist the help of parents immediately?

_____ Are there established procedures for dealing with parents' demands, especially those of a vocal minority?

_____ Other?

Principle 5: Outreach to All Families

_____ Is there a policy for informing non-custodial parents about their children's performance and school events?

_____ Do teachers sometimes meet outside school hours with parents who have jobs and cannot easily get away during the working day?

_____ Does the school hold evening and weekend events for its families so that employed parents (mothers, fathers, others) can come to see the school?

_____ If there is a substantial minority language population at the school; are written communications provided in that language?

_____ Is in-service training offered for teachers on how to deal with problems caused by divorce, separation, or imprisonment, such as how to avoid being caught between warring parents, or the impact of family breakup on children?

_____ Are there any special programs, such as peer group discussions, for students whose parents are separating, divorced, imprisoned, or deceased?

_____ Is there an outreach program for parents—especially minority parents—who do not participate at all in school events, (e.g., in which faculty or parent volunteers are willing to make home visits or attend church meetings to answer questions, allay fears, and explain the importance of being involved in their children's education)?

_____ When a particular parent refuses to cooperate with the principal or teacher, is there a school staff member trained to intervene and work with that parent?

_____ Other?

Principle 6: Promoting a Philosophy of Partnership

_____ Does the school have a written statement about partnership with parents that is clearly available, especially in all written publications?

_____ Are there in-service opportunities for training teachers to work with parents?

_____ Is time at staff meetings devoted to discussing working with parents and reinforcing efforts of teachers' and parents?

_____ Are teachers encouraged to consult with the principal if they are having difficulty dealing with a parent?

_____ Does the principal offer to sit in at meetings with teachers and parents or to mediate any dispute between them?

_____ Does the principal substitute in the classroom or make substitutes available to allow teachers and other staff to have meetings with parents?

_____ Does the school offer assistance to help parents with babysitting, transportation, or other logistical difficulties, so they can attend school events?

_____ Are space, staff support and resources, (i.e., reasonable access to a copy machine, computer services, a desk, etc.) provided for parents' school-related activities?

_____ Other?

Principle 7: Volunteer Participation

_____ Does the school have an organized volunteer program with a coordinator (paid or volunteer)?

_____ Does the program draw from retired people, the business community, local citizens, and students as well as parents?

_____ Is there a wide variety of jobs available for volunteers, including those that could be done at home or on weekends?

_____ Are all parents expected to volunteer in some way during the school year?

_____ Is the program reassessed periodically, with the participation of parents, teachers, and other volunteers, to ensure that the program is meeting school needs effectively?

_____ Are local businesses and community organizations contacted to provide learning opportunities outside the school and to explore career options for high-school students?

_____ Has a local business (or other institutions) been asked to "adopt" your school?

_____ Other?

Phase Two.   The following suggested activities are designed to help you complete a final assessment of your host school's family–school relationships, especially from the perspective of the many barriers that face parents in their attempts to become more involved in their children's education.

1. Take a snapshot or draw a picture of the entrance to the school. Examine it carefully. Does the school look inviting, friendly, and homey? How do you think that parents of different cultural or class groups would tend to "read" the school entrance? What architectural features present physical barriers between parents and schools?

2. Now, take a second snapshot or draw a picture of the school's main office. Examine it carefully. Does the school's main office look inviting and friendly? Is there a special room for parents at the school? Does anyone in the school have a special assignment to make parents feel welcome? How were you greeted when you came into the office? Is there any official protocol established in the school to deal with parental visits? Are translators available for parents who do not speak English? What are parents and other visitors required to do when they enter the school? Sit in the office for an hour. Make note of the interaction between parents and school personnel.

3. Make a list of all the special events held at the school during the year that include parents. When are these events held? How are they advertised? Are parents invited individually? Is child care and transportation provided for these events? How does the school communicate with the parents? What messages do school policies give to parents about their acceptance in the daily life of school? Are some groups of parents more welcome in the school than other groups? How does the scheduling of open houses, PTA meetings, and conferences prevent some parents from being more involved in the school?

4. Attend a PTA meeting. Make a tally by both race and gender of those who attend. Find out how PTA officers are elected. In what activities

is the PTA involved? Interview the head of the PTA and ask her or him to construct a similar list of the ways that she or he conceptualizes the idea of parental involvement.

Reflective Narrative

Now look more critically at the information that you have gathered. Have any of your findings surprised you? On a separate page, make a list of the areas you determine to be special strengths at the schools and those that need more work. Discuss your findings with a school administrator.

Related Readings

Comer, J. P. (1980). *Schoolpower: Implications of an intervention project*. New York: The Free Press.

Daher, J. (1994). School–parent partnerships: A guide. In C. Fagnano & B. Werber (Eds.), *School, family, and community interaction: A view from the firing lines* (pp. XX–XX). Boulder, CO: Westview Press.

Henderson, A. T. (1986). *Beyond the bake sale: An educator's guide to working with parents*. Washington, DC: National Committee for Citizens in Education.

Ryan, B. A., Adams, G. R., Gullotta, T., Weissberg, R., & Hampton, R. (Eds.) (1995). *The family–school connection: Theory, research, and practice*. Thousand Oaks, CA: Sage.

Winters, W. C. (1993). *African American mothers and urban schools: The power of participation*. New York: Lexington Books.

ASSESSING THE PARENT–TEACHER RELATIONSHIP

Background

The involvement of parents in the school has been found to to be an important indicator of student success.[33] Recent educational research studies have overwhelmingly confirmed the psychological, social, and academic benefits of greater parental involvement and participation at every level of children's elementary, middle, and high-school education.[34] Given the demands of parental work schedules today (regardless of social class), most parents find it difficult (if not impossible) to be physically involved in their children's schools, especially during normal school hours. Research also shows, however, that parents of all social classes want to be more involved in their children's education but seek more direction from the classroom teacher.[35] Teachers themselves feel ambivalent about the wisdom of encouraging greater parental involvement in the schools, and only about 47% of inner city teachers surveyed believed in strong family involvement.[36] As a result, schools have begun to see the value of more in-service teacher education programs focusing on parental involvement and have begun to experiment with many innovative and creative parental involvement programs and practices.

In the following exercise you will be invited to examine the nature and scope of parent–teacher relationships at your host school from the perspective of the many barriers that parents face. Consider the following questions. Despite the growing body of research literature that catalogs the effectiveness of parental involvement programs, are the parent–teacher connections at your host school either nonexistent or confined to periodic, superficial "displays" of parental support (i.e., the annual PTA meeting, meet-the-teacher nights, and end-of-year awards ceremonies)? Are there any school and teacher practices that deter further parental involvement? What is meant by the term "parental involvement" at your host school?

Activity

The following checklist developed by the staff at the National Committee for Citizens in Education lists some new parental involvement initiatives and provides a diagnostic questionnaire that you can use to evaluate how well your host school is fostering healthy parent–teacher relationships.[37]

Assessing Parent–Teacher Relationships Checklist (Answer "yes" or "no")

Principle 1: Classroom Climate

_____ Are parent observers welcome in the classroom?

_____ Are there any adult-size chairs besides the teacher's?

_____ Is the classroom organized so that a parent can see easily what happens in it?

_____ Are examples of every child's work displayed regularly?

_____ Is the classroom routine written down and clearly posted?

_____ Are socioeconomically poor parents worked with from an empowerment rather than a deficit model of parental involvement?

_____ Other?

Principle 2: Communication

_____ Are parents informed at the beginning of the year how they can reach the teacher?

_____ Does the teacher tell parents about good things as well as problems?

_____ Does the teacher try to communicate at least once a month with each parent (less often in high school, but regularly)?

_____ Does the teacher talk to parents in person (or on the phone), in addition to sending written messages?

_____ Does the teacher provide regular opportunities for parents to see their child's written work?

_____ Does the teacher let parents know about expectations for homework, grading policies, and how parents can help?

_____ Does the teacher let parents know what information about the child is needed to help teachers do a better job (e.g., family stress or major changes in family: illness, birth, death, divorce, etc.)?

_____ Does the teacher praise parents regularly in front of peers at group meetings?

_____ Other?

Principle 3: Parents as Collaborators

_____ Do teachers ask parents for their advice on how to deal with their children?

_____ Is there an early warning system for notifying parents if a student is falling behind or having social problems so the teacher may confer with them about the situation?

_____ Before parents are informed about a serious problem, are other school staff consulted to gather their perspectives on the student?

_____ Are parents encouraged to advise teachers when a child is exhibiting a learning or school adjustment difficulty at home?

_____ In suggesting ways that parents can help at home, does the teacher take into account a student's particular cultural background and home situation?

_____ Do teachers make it clear to parents that parents must respect teachers' need for time alone and with their own families?

_____ Do teachers help parents understand that their child's needs must be balanced with those of the whole class?

_____ Are parents employed in the classrooms as teacher's aides? tutors? counselors? chaperons? hall monitors? or assistants in the computer labs or library?

_____ Are parents invited to speak to the class about their careers, their hobbies, and the like?

_____ Other?

Principle 4: Parents as Advisors and Decision Makers

_____ Are parents with questions and ideas about school policy encouraged to play an active role in the school as members of advisory boards?

_____ Do teachers attend parent–teacher organization meetings regularly?

_____ Do teachers listen actively to parents' concerns and pass them on to the principal or the parent–teacher organization president?

_____ Do teachers make it clear that some decisions about a child are not negotiable (e.g., grades, promotions, etc.)?

_____ Other?

Principle 5: Outreach to All Families

_____ Are teachers adequately trained and supported in their dealings with the

_____ problems of divorced or separated families?

_____ Do teachers make special efforts to reach families from other cultures (e.g., home visits, translators, etc.)?

_____ Do teachers meet outside regular school hours, if necessary, with parents who are employed?

_____ Are teachers persistent in their efforts to reach parents who try to avoid coming to school?

_____ Do teachers invite parents to eat breakfast and lunch with their children at school?

_____ Other?

Principle 6: Volunteers

_____ Do teachers use volunteers creatively (both parents and other citizens) to meet needs in the classroom?

_____ Do teachers expect every parent to help in some way, and are parents offered a variety of ways to do so?

_____ Other?

Reflective Narrative

What further implications and recommendations might you draw from your findings. The report, *A Nation of Risk*,[38] and other similar reform documents tend to acknowledge the primacy of parental participation in "the work of the schools," emphasizing the role of parents in the achievement of national- and state-level curriculum content, subject standards, disciplinary ex-

pectations, skill basics, and standardized testing. By contrast, Joyce Epstein, at the Center for Research on Effective Schooling for Disadvantaged Students, has argued thus:

[P]erhaps the ideal situation for children's education and development occurs, when-school–family distinctions become blurred—when schools become more family-like and families become more school-like.[39]

Jane Roland Martin presented the imagery of the "schoolhome," a place characterized by "safety, security, nurturance, and love ... [and] guided by a spirit of family-like affection."[40] Which model characterizes the school climate at your host school? Do you agree or disagree with Epstein's and Martin's images for the American school? Why or why not? What is your vision of the ideal teacher–parent relationship?

Related Readings

Comer, J. P. (1980). *Schoolpower: Implications of an intervention project*. New York: The Free Press.

Henderson, A. T. (1986). *Beyond the bake sale: An educator's guide to working with parents*. Washington, DC: National Committee for Citizens in Education.

Morrow, R. D. (1991). The challenge of Southeast Asian parental involvement. *Principal*, January, 20–22.

Noddings, Nel. (1992). *The challenge to care in schools: An alternative approach to education*. New York: Teachers College Press.

Winter, W. C. (1993). *African-American mothers and urban schools: The power of participation*. New York: Lexington Books.

SCHOOL-TO-WORK LINKAGES

Background

There are few more controversial issues today in U.S. education than the role of the schools in preparing students for the world of work. This is not as much a problem for upwardly mobile middle-class, college-bound youngsters as it is for poor, minority, at-risk students. The latter students many times feel a hopelessness about never having the kind of job that will provide them with stable employment and the resources to provide for a secure family household. Current labor force analyses highlight the difficulties encountered by these young people in making the transition from school to work.[41]

The scarcity of stable, low-credentialed employment in the United States has made it almost impossible for these students to find good-paying career jobs right after high school. Research reveals that they tend to spend several years floundering in the labor market, and many do not succeed in finding steady work until the age of 40 years.[42] These concerns, along with the extraordinary workplace benefits and salary differentials of workers with college degrees, have raised serious questions about the kind of vocational education programs that we should be planning for the 21st century.

David Stern and his associates[43] classified school-to-work programs into two categories: school-for-work programs (i.e., the older, more traditional vocational education programs) and "school-and-work" programs (i.e., the newer programs that have been more comprehensively integrated with the academic school curricula).

The school-for-work programs generally are those vocational programs funded under the Smith–Hughes Act of 1917 that emphasize the need to train workers in the industrial intelligence and mechanical skills needed by routine, assembly-line production systems. These school-for-work programs have long suffered from the reputation of being the dumping grounds for children experiencing difficulty with the regular classroom academic programs (i.e., academically underachieving students, resistant lower-class minority children with behavior problems, and mentally challenged students). When the dramatic loss in manufacturing jobs took place in the late 1970s and early 1980s, these school-for-work programs shifted from a manufacturing emphasis to that of training youth for the emerging fast-food, transportation, and restaurant enterprises.[44]

Some would argue that although these new service sector jobs are unsuitable for college-bound, middle-class youth (except on a temporary basis), they are "ideal" for lower-class, nonacademic youth. Indeed, minorities are highly represented in these occupations (more than 22% of employees in eating establishments are Black or Hispanic). From another perspective, however, it is argued that these jobs provide little opportunity for job mobility and little room for initiative, creativity, or individual expression. Etizoni wrote that these "fast-food franchises are breeding grounds for robots working for yesterday's assembly lines and not practice fields for committed workers in tomorrow's high-tech posts."[45] Not only do these workplaces provide meager income and few useful job skills for these youth, but they also tend to perpetuate their disadvantaged status: Such jobs provide no career incentives and few marketable skills.[46] No wonder there is growing concern among vocational educators about what and how they are teaching these students.

Data suggest that although this older model of vocational education is still the predominant model used in American schools, there is a shift toward the newer school-and-work programs. The Carl D. Perkins Vocational and Applied Technology Education Act of 1990 called for the integration of vocational and academic education through school-and-work programs that allow students to work and attend class during the same time period. Cooperative education, new youth apprenticeships, and school-based enterprises are the major examples of these work programs being offered to students in many high schools and secondary vocational centers. The most positive aspect of such programs is that academic skills, critical-thinking skills, and problem-solving skills are considered equally important as any specific occupational skill training. There is also a priority that these programs provide students with the academic credentials to pursue either college-level studies or types of postsecondary education.[47]

Activity

Investigate the vocational education programs at your host school. Note the defining characteristics of the students in these classes. What can you conclude about the age, race, ethnicity, sex, and academic characteristics of these students?

Speak with some of the vocational education teachers about their programs and their students. Have they seen a shift in emphasis in the programs over the past 10 years? If so, what has been the nature of the changes in the programs? What has been the impact of these programs on the students? Are they satisfied with the vocational education program at their school? What would they do to improve it?

Find out how many of the following strategies are currently being used at the school in which you are doing your classroom observations to prepare all students better for the school to work transition.

Reflective Narrative

Although applauding the direction of these newer vocational education programs, with their increased concern for the academic as well as applied vocational and technology programs, some critical theorists are concerned that vocational education students still lack the kind of entry-level knowledge and skills needed to ensure that they can "interject their social and moral imaginations into the refashioning of work—where workplace ethnics, economics, and politics are defined not by cultural elites, but by a consensus of the whole."[49] Lakes argued strongly for a "critical education for work" that would enable future vocational education students to reexamine the assumptions on which their programs rest. What do you think are the components of a critical education for work for vocational education students?

Related Readings

Borman, K. (1991). *The first "real" job: A study of young workers.* Albany: State University of New York Press.

Lakes, R. D. (Ed.). (1994). *Critical education and work: Multidisciplinary approaches.* Norwood, NJ: Ablex.

Law, C. J., Knuth, R. A. , & Bergman, S. (1992). *What does research say about school-to-work transition?* Oak Brook, IL: NCREL; Electric Library, WWW.

Rifkin, J. (1995). *The end of work: The decline of the global labor force and the dawn of the post-market era.* New York: Putnam.

Simon, R. I., Dippo, D., & Schenke, A. (1991). *Learning work: A critical pedagogy of work education.* New York: Bergin & Garvey.

Survey of School-to-Work Linkages[48]

	YES	NO
1. Opportunities for all students and teachers to learn outside of school		
2. Opportunities for all students to have access to adults in the community as role models, tutors, aides, and/or as mentors		
3. Opportunities for all students to provide community services such as community volunteer work, environmental clean-up, and the like		
4. Opportunities for all students to participate in local community business and organizational clubs		
5. Opportunities for all students to hear guest speakers from the community discuss the nature of their occupations and provisions for follow-up visits to these local community businesses and corporate centers to see these skills in operation in the real world		
6. Opportunities for all students to investigate, via class projects and other activities, local businesses, industries, and service sector agencies to familiarize themselves with jobs and work environments		
7. Apprenticeships spanning secondary and postsecondary education		
8. Tech-prep programs, school-based enterprises, co-op programs		
9. Evidence that critical education-for-work skills are being taught to the vocational education students		
10. Development of advanced skills technical curriculum		
11. Job placement and counseling services for students; on-campus interviews		
12. College linkages established for college credit academic/applied technology and vocational education courses		
13. Joint in-service workshops for secondary/post-secondary personnel (e.g., faculty, counselors, administrators, etc.) involved in technology/vocational education programs		
14. Vocational programs that integrate vocational and rigorous academic curriculum (also, evidence that critical thinking and problem-solving skills are being taught)		
15. Careers days, career information workshops		

EXTRACURRICULAR SCHOOL ACTIVITIES

Background

In studies of schooling and youth culture in the United States, the role and function of extracurricular school activities has been a rich subject for historical and sociological study. Although researchers are divided on their analyses of the function that extracurricular activities has played and continues to play in the larger community life of the nation, there is little disagreement that extracurricular school activities do contribute to the development and reinforcement of a wide array of physical, emotional, social, academic, aesthetic, and spiritual dimensions of a young child. In addition to the feeling of belonging, so important for children, extracurricular school activities take the place of negative peer influences and "the TV-till-bedtime routine" so common among many American children.

In recent historic studies, O'Hanlon,[50] Spring,[51] Violas,[52] and others[53] have researched the history of extracurricular sports in U.S. schools. They discovered that Progressive Era extracurricular school activities were initially adopted into the public school curriculum to fill the vacant time (especially of poor urban children) with supervised after-school activities designed to reinforce the new group-oriented, assembly-line industrial work habits and attitudes (i.e., group competition, unequal rewards, hard work, etc.) in working-class, immigrant children. In his research, Spring[54] emphasized "the unification function" that extracurricular activities played in the new comprehensive high schools by creating a dominant school cultural ethos characterized by "school spirit," teamwork, and "working for the good of the whole." He

questioned whether extracurricular school activities do or should play such a role in the public school systems. In addition, some concern exists that such programs mitigate feelings of class consciousness or tendencies toward social class conflict in the schools in light of the concomitant adoption and implementation by school administrators of hierarchical systems of student academic tracking and standardized testing.

Today, the issue of extracurricular school activities is problematic and subject to varying interpretations. Sociologists are divided on the present role and function that extracurricular sports activities play in today's school culture.[55] Some believe that films, television, Nintendo, video arcades, and computer games have taken the place of extracurricular sports for many youngsters. Others believe that nothing has really replaced the character-building potential of extracurricular sports and that increased teenage violence and crime rates may be directly related to our neglect of the centrality that extracurricular sports should have for all our children, not just the elite few.

Given the renewed emphasis on "the basics" combined with increasingly financially strapped school districts, many schools are now curtailing extracurricular school activities as unnecessary frills. Increasing numbers of high-school students are involved in after-school service sector jobs until late in the evening.[56] In many schools, too, after-school activities have died a slow death—largely because of scheduling conflicts with buses, general student apathy, and the growing tendency to professionalize after-school activities.[57] It is crucial, therefore, that the beginning teacher educator examine the status, vitality, and breadth of extracurricular school activities at their host schools.

Activity

What extracurricular activities did you participate in when you were in high school? Describe the students who participated with you in these activities by social class, gender, and race or ethnicity.

Using the chart from Fig 4.4, make a list of all the extracurricular activities available to students at the school. Get a list of times and places that each team, club, or activity meets. Make an attempt to attend at least one meeting of each school team, club, or activity. During the meeting, make some notes about the composition of the club in terms of the students' perceived social class, racial, ethnic, gender, or academic-track characteristics. Attempt to solicit some qualitative comments from the participants about why they joined this particular club and whether other members of their peer group also joined the club.

Reflective Narrative

Phase One

1. On the basis of your notes, what general conclusions might you draw about the status, vitality, inclusive nature, and breadth of extracurricular activities at your school.

2. Check your impressions with one of the school administrators. What recommendations might you make to the school administration to ensure more equitable participation by all races, genders, and ability classes in each extracurricular activity? Develop your own rationale for the importance of extracurricular sports and school activities.

Phase Two.   Now, review the survey data you have generated regarding extracurricular activities at your school from a more critical and analytic perspective. How do you explain the similarities or differences that you found from the school you attended as a child? In drawing your comparisons, ask yourself the following questions:

1. Who participates in extracurricular activities at your host school? Do you think there might be a hidden set of rules and assumptions about who should show up for certain sports or specific after-school activities at the school? Thus, is there an issue of access and students' perceptions about the race, ethnicity, gender, physical makeup, academic credentials, social status, and so on of the students likely to be accepted if they show up for certain activities?

2. Do extracurricular activities tend to be class based at your host school? Often, extracurricular sports activities function only to reproduce the same social class and ethnic differences evident in the school's academic tracking systems (i.e., nerds in newspaper club; jocks in sports clubs; middle class in large group activities—band, service club, etc.; ivy leaguers in solo sports—swimming, kayaking, chess; etc.) Is this the case at the school?

3. What groups do not participate in extracurricular activities at your host school? It is also important to notice what groups are routinely missing from any kind of participation in extracurricular sports (e.g., the greasers, the punks, the druggies, the skinheads, the at-risk, students etc). This disaffected population of potential dropouts often form their own after-school groups. What might the school do to include these groups in some meaningful after-school activities?

Related Readings

Larkin, R. W. (1979). *Suburban youth in cultural crisis.* New York: Oxford University Press.

O-Hanlon, T. (1980). Interscholastic Athletics, 1900–1940: Shaping citizens for unequal roles in the modern industrial state. *Educational Theory, 30*(2), 89–103, Spring.

Sedlak, M., Wheeler, C., Pullin, D., & Cusick, P. (Eds.). (1986). *Selling students short: Classroom bargains and academic reform in the American high school.* New York: Teachers College Press.

Spring, J. (1972). *Education and the rise of the corporate liberal state.* Boston: Beacon Press.

Violas, P. (1978). *The training of the urban working class: A history of twentieth century American education* (pp. 93–123). Chicago: Rand McNally College Publishing Company.

Activities	# Enrolled	% Males	% Females	Frequency of Meetings
1. Athletic Teams/Clubs				
2. Bank/Orchestra				
3. Choir/Choral Clubs				
4. Career-Oriented Clubs				
5. Language Clubs				
6. Drama/Theater				
7. Pep Club				
8. School Publications				
9. Student Council/Government				
10. Service/Volunteer Groups				
11. National Honor Societies				
12. Debate/Speech				
13. Cheerleading				
14. Science Clubs				
15. Other				
16. Other				
17. Other				

FIG 4.4. Student participation in school-related activities (reproduce as needed).

REBELLION, CONFORMITY, AND "MAKING DUE"

Background

School is the place in which peer groups begin to form and be shaped in terms of their relationship to the dominant school culture. Most schools track, stream, or group children on the basis of their perceived ability almost from the day they enter the school door. The detrimental impact of these practices on children is by now well established: No matter how high the achievement of the lower track children, they almost always feel like dummies or failures. These ability groupings also appear to be critical in the formation of friendship groups. Study after study shows that these childhood friendship groups (cliques) almost always form among students who study together or share a common academic track.[58]

In this exercise, we attempt to capture some of the feelings and drama of American children as they struggle through the public school system. We aim to identify what happens to students through the process of school socialization. What are their struggles? What are their survival strategies? We must remember that even in the most oppressive top-down management of educational bureaucracies, each child still has some power of choice as to how he or she will respond to the school organizational structure, culture, and values. Webb and Sherman argued that children have three significant options in that "they can conform to the institution, rebel against it, or adopt a crafty middle position we shall call 'making due.'"[59] A careful observation of school life in classrooms, hallways, restrooms, lunchroom, outdoors, parking lot, gym, and the like will reveal the active and dynamic nature of these school subcultural groups. In the activities that follow, we examine the implications and consequences of these various student options: conformity, resistance, and making due.

The Conformist Student

Students who conform to the expectations of the school, internalize school values, align themselves with the institution, promote school spirit, and work to become active members in school organizations and clubs are usually labeled as model students. What are the skills such individuals master on their way to becoming model students?

The Rebellious Student

In most schools, there are members who actively resist the roles they are expected to play and thus rarely experience "success" in school. Some researchers contend that this is because their cultures ill prepare them for life in schools, whereas others argue that such rebellion is a healthy response to an institution that denies them self-esteem, cultural expression, or racial identity. What can you observe about the character and motivation of rebellious students at your school?

The "Making Due" Student

In his research, Goffman found that within institutions, individuals who decline to accept the official view of how the organization should function tend to make "second adjustments."[60] In other words, many students within large educational bureaucracies seek out subtle ways to recoup their individuality and sense of self. Such students do not totally conform to the institutional ethos as do the model students, but neither do they openly resist it. Webb argued that the in-school existence of such students is defined by a daily search "to make due," to subtlely express their individuality within the confines of a coercive school system. See how many of these "making due" behaviors you can identify at your host school. For example, do you see any of the behaviors or situations at your host school identified in the chart from Fig 4.5?[61]

Reflective Narrative

1. Interview several students about the peer groups and cliques within their schools. With the help of these students, make a chart to illustrate the status hierarchy of these school groups. Which groups hold the most power? How does this power get translated into privileges within and outside the school? Classify each of the school groups according to the three categories: conformity, rebellion, or "making due." What conclusions or implications can you draw as a result of this activity? How do these peer groups compare with the groups that existed when you were in high school?

2. View one of the following films:

Boyz n the Hood

Lean on Me

Dead Poets Society

Stand and Deliver

Do the Right Thing

School Ties

Hoop Dreams

Dangerous Minds

Blackboard Jungle

Make a list of all the classroom-related behaviors you see exhibited in the film. Categorize each behavior you listed into one of the three options presented by Webb and Sherman: conformity, rebellion, or "making due." Can you develop some categories of your own to categorize the school-related behaviors you observe?

Related Readings

Farrell, E. (1990). *Hanging in and dropping out: Voice of at-risk high school students.* New York: Teachers College Press.

Fordman, S. (1993). Those loud Black girls: (Black) women, silence, and gender "passing" in the academy. *Anthropology and Education Quarterly, 24* (1), 3–32.

Roman, L. G., & Christian-Smith, L. (1988). *Becoming feminine: The politics of popular culture.* London: Falmer Press.

Virgil, J. D. (1988). *Barrio gangs: Street life and identity in Southern California.* Austin: University of Texas Press.

Webb, R., & Sherman, R. (1989). *Schooling and society.* (pp. 307–322). New York: Macmillan.

Willis, P. (1978). *Learning to labor: How working class kids get working class jobs.* Lexington, MA: D.C. Heath.

"Making Due" Classroom Situations	YES		NO
1. Use of school facilities for "illicit" purposes (e.g., smoking, lovemaking, etc.).			
2. Efforts to slow down/circumvent work in classroom (e.g., complaining, copying homework, etc.).			
3. Alternative communication networks (e.g., notes, whispering, pagers, etc.).			
4. Body/facial management (e.g., daydreaming, pretended interest, frantic hand-raising, etc.).			
5. Currying artificial favor with teacher/"the apple polishers."			
6. Classroom invisibility (e.g., sitting in back of the room, never volunteering).			
7. Responding with words/tone of voice that is ambiguous (e.g., teacher finds it difficult to challenge a subtly rebellious student).			
8. Covert school vandalism/abuse of school property (e.g., subtle disregard for and petty damage to school property and classroom materials).			
9. Others? Can you observe any other "making do" behaviors at your school?			
10. Others?			

FIG 4.5. Observing "making due" Classroom Situations (reproduce as needed).

VIOLENT OR SAFE SCHOOLS: POLICE AND MILITARY LINKAGES

Background

Recent studies have shown a disturbing correlation between increases in unemployment and the rise in violent crime.[62] Rising unemployment and loss of hope for a better future are among the reasons that tens of thousands of teenagers are turning to a life of crime and violence. Attorney General Reno called youth violence "the greatest single crime problem in America today."[63] In 1992, nearly 1,000,000 young people between the ages of 12 and 14 years were "raped, robbed, or assaulted, often by their peers."[64] Indeed, there is little doubt that America has become a more dangerous place for a young person to live, and the American public school system has likewise become a more dangerous place to work. Consider the following statistics:

- US citizens possess more than 200,000,000 guns: 73,000,000 rifles, 66,000,000 handguns, and 62,000,000 shotguns.
- In 1990, handguns murdered 10 people in Australia, 22 in Great Britain, 68 in Canada, and 10,567 in the United States.
- The average U.S. child witnesses 8,000 murders and 100,000 other acts of violence on TV by the time he or she has finished elementary school.
- Police estimate that more than 270,000 students carry guns to school every day in the United States.
- A recent study by the Harvard School of Public Health found that 59% of children in the 6th through 12th grades said they could get a handgun if they wanted one.

- More than 3,000,000 crimes occur every year on school grounds.[65]

Given these statistics, it is understandable why the creation of a safe and orderly school environment has become a major research and media emphasis in recent school reform efforts. A growing body of research suggests that school practices can be effective in dealing with these disruptive student behaviors. The research is divided, however, on the causes and probable solutions to this recent rapid escalation of school violence and criminal activity.[66]

The Police Model of School Security

Proponents of this model argue that school violence has resulted from the growing presence of criminal and gang-related activities within the public school grounds. They recommend the installation of massive electronic surveillance and security systems. This police model of school security recommends the following measures in response to increased school violence and destruction of school property:

1. Increased high-tech surveillance (e.g., video cameras, metal detectors, two-way radios, mirrors, x-ray machines, phones in classrooms, closed-circuit TV, etc.)
2. Tougher discipline (e.g., imposing stricter dress codes, requiring school uniforms, creating "zero tolerance" schools, etc.)
3. Increased student locker searches and use of drug-detecting dogs
4. Creation of gun-free school zones and use of student photo ID systems

5. More school security personnel, including school police, probation officers, school-linked police. (The New York City school system now operates the 11th largest security force in the United States, with more than 2,400 officers.)
6. Tougher punishment (e.g., more school infractions that require suspension and expulsion proceedings) and tighter connections with the juvenile court system
7. Increased use of "yellow-code alerts" alongside fire drills so children learn to "hit the deck when the bullets fly"[67]
8. School security as a school goal alongside academic achievement[68]

The Ecology/Climate Model of School Security

By contrast, the ecology/climate model of school security frames school security within the wider context of overcrowded classrooms, school segregation, student poverty, and racial tension. This approach to school security argues that when educators blame only youth gangs for school violence, they prevent themselves from seeking a more comprehensive approach to creating a truly safe and academic learning environment. In contrast to the police model that focuses on the characteristics of counterculture school groups, the ecology model emphasizes the importance of improving the learning environment by concentrating on the school's climate, wellness, culture, and organizational features. For example, the National Institute of Education report[69] recommended the following measures to eliminate school violence:

1. Reinforce the vision that all students can learn, study, and work peacefully together. Care and consideration must be extended to each person within the school environment.
2. School processes, practices, and organizational structures need to provide a strong learning environment free of racial tension or discrimination based on race, gender, language, and the like.

3. School restructuring needs to encourage greater use of student and administrative dialogues, greater voice for students in the school's operation, and increased student participation in all aspects of school decision making.
4. A sense of community must be developed; parental and neighborhood ties must be strengthened; parents must be made partners and decision makers in every aspect of the school's operation.
5. School facilities must be better maintained and upgraded.[70]

Activity

Study the model of school security in operation at your school. Does it resemble the police model or the ecology/climate model? Discuss each of these models with members of the school administration. Get their views on why they prefer and use one rather than the other.

Reflective Narrative

Politicians are known for finding and using statistics that justify whatever social policy they choose to support. The crime statistics are no exception, especially as they relate to increased rates of school violence, gang-related school activities, and school property damage. Put yourself in the role of a critically skeptical educational researchers. Is there any way you can independently verify or critique the statistics presented in this exercise? Are there any more up-to-date sources that might change one's perspective on these issues? (Hint: You might want to consult the following internet sites: Center for the Prevention of School Violence and/or SchoolNet.)

Related Readings

Curcio, J. L., & First, P. F. (1993). *Violence in the schools: How to proactively prevent and defuse it.* Newbury Park, CA: Corwin Press.

Goodwille, S. (Ed.). (1993). *Voices from the future: Our children tell us about violence in America.* New York: Crown.

National Institute of Education. (1978). *Violent schools—safe schools: The safe school study, report to Congress, Volume I.* Washington, DC: Government Printing Office.

National School Board Association. (1994). *Violence in our schools: How America's school boards are*

safeguarding your children. Washington, DC: Author.

Quarles, C. L. (1993). *Staying safe at school.* Thousand Oaks, CA: Corwin Press.

CYBERSPACE AND THE VIRTUAL CLASSROOM

Background

Computer-mediated communication systems are believed to have powerful effects on social relationships. Many claim that this new form of social interaction encourages wider participation, greater honesty in dialogue, and an emphasis on merit over status. In short, the belief is that old social hierarchies are dissolved and that flatter, more egalitarian social organizations emerge in cyberspace. Networked communications, it is argued, have ushered in a renewed era of democratic participation and revitalized community.[71] But as with earlier technologies that promised freedom and power, the central problems of relationships remain, although in new and possibly more challenging forms. Will "electronic democracy" be an accurate description of an emerging new mode/tool of politically empowering discourse for students or will it become just another technological tool of "disinfotainment," another means of manipulating emotions and manufacturing public opinion in the service of power? Who will control? Who will censor? Who will communicate with whom in this new virtual community?

The impact of this new computer-mediated environment on American educational institutions has barely begun to be addressed. Recent studies suggest, however, that the impact will be dramatic, and in fact, has already begun to be felt in literally every classroom around the country.[72] Linking up with "the information superhighway" has become the buzzword of every school administrator, and becoming part of the world wide web (WWW) has become the new golden goose promising finally to herald in the new age of high technology. In his book, *Virtual Reality*,[73] Howard Reingold reviewed some of the impact that this new medium of communication is potentially envisioned to have on classrooms and learning in the next century. A virtual community, Reingold explained, is a group of people who meet via computer-mediated communication and who exchange words and ideas through computer bulletin boards, home pages, chat rooms, and instant messages. Students connected to the Internet, Reingold told us, will chat and argue, engage in intellectual discussions, share emotional support, make plans, brainstorm, gossip, feud, fall in love, do homework together, find friends, play games, engage in a lot of idle talk, and exchange information, knowledge, and resources.[44]

Activity

Observe students in schools using computers online. What are they doing? What sites are they visiting? Are they communicating with others around the world? Are they simply using the computer like an encyclopedia? Talk with them about what they like and dislike about the Internet.

Reflective Narrative

On the basis of your observations, write a short reflective narrative indicating why you agree or disagree with the following poem, "Mind-On-Line: The First Noble Truth" by Mitchell Kapor:

> This is the First Noble Truth of cyberspace:
> We bring our baggage with us.
> All the ways of being what we are,
> as individuals and as a society—

whether enthusiastic, idealistic,
romantic, naive, ambitious, impatient,
practical, bigoted, selfish—
all will manifest themselves
in the nonmaterial reality
called cyberspace.
It is a non-space where
people come together
not in body, but through words alone.
Because cyberspace
strips away markers of
age, sex, race, and class,
all of which heavily shape
our social interactions,
one might think it provides
a completely neutral space
where we are devoid of self
and can engage with each other
in a wholly fresh, unmediated way.
The First Truth gives the lie
to this charming but naive notion.
We seem bound to use whatever cues we can
    find,
however slight, to guide us.[75]

—Mitchell Kapor,
Adj. Prof/MIT
Founder, Lotus Development Corporation
(designed Lotus 1-2-3)
Chairman, Electronic Frontier Foundation
(until 1995)

Related Readings

Benedikt, M. (Ed.). (1991). *Cyberspace: First steps.* Cambridge, MA: MIT Press.

Gergen, K. J. (1991). *The saturated self.* New York: Basic Books.

Jones, S. (Ed.). (1995). *Cybersociety: Computer-mediated communication and community.* Thousand Oaks, CA: Sage.

Kramarae, C. (Ed.). (1991). *Technology and women's voices.* New York: Routledge & Kegan Paul.

Reingold, H. (1993). *The virtual community: Homesteading on the electronic frontier.* Reading, MA: Addison-Wesley.

Turkle, S. (1995). *Life on the screen: Identity in the age of the Internet.* New York: Simon & Schuster.

NOTES

[1]Bobbitt, F. (1913). *The supervision of city schools: Some general principles of management applied to the problems of city school systems.* Twelfth Yearbook, Part I, National Society for the Study of education. Bloomington, IN: Public School Publishing Company, p. 1.

[2]Ross, E. (1906). *Social control,* cited in Karier, C. J., Violas, P., & Spring, J. (Eds.) Roots of crisis: American education in the twentieth century (p. 32). Chicago: Rand McNally College Publishing.

[3]Heilbroner, R. (1980), p. 175; cited in Orr, D. W. (1992). *Ecological literacy: education and the transition to a post-modern world.* Albany: State University of New York Press.

[4]de Chardin, T. (1965). pp. 43–44; cited in Miller, J. (1993). *The holistic curriculum.* Ontario, Canada: OISE Press, p. 76.

[5]Apple, M., & Beane, J. A. (Eds.). (1995). *Democratic schools.* Washington, DC: Association for Curriculum and Development; Smyth, J. (Ed). (1993). *A socially critical view of the self-managed school.* Washington, DC: Falmer Press; David, J. (1989). Synthesis of research on school based management. *Educational Leadership, 71* (1), 45–53; Karier, C. J. (1986). *The individual, society, and education: A history of American educational ideas* (2nd ed.). (pp. 286–362). Urbana: University of Illinois Press; Spring J. (1996). *American education* (7th ed.). New York: McGraw-Hill.

[6]Smyth, J. (Ed.). (1993). *A socially critical view of the self-managed school.* Washington, DC: Falmer Press, p. 3.

[7]Whitmyer, C. (Ed.). (1993). *In the company of others: Making community in the modern world.* New York: Jeremy P. Tarcher/Perigee Books, p. xx.

[8]Smyth, J. (Ed.). (1993). *A socially critical view of he self-managed school.* Washington, DC: Falmer Press, 35–48 passim.

[9]McDaniel, T. R. (1989). Demilitarizing public education: School reform in the era of George Bush. *Phi Delta Kappan, 42*(2), 15–18.

[10]Shea, C. M., Kahane, E., & Sola, P. (Eds.). (1989). *The new servants of power: A critique of the 1980s educational reform movement.* Westport, CT: Greenwood, pp. 12–16, passim.

[11]Kozol, J. (1991). *Savage inequalities: Children in America's schools.* New York: Crown.

[12]Orr, D. W. (1992). *Ecological literacy: Education and the transition to a post-modern world.* Albany: State University of New York Press.

[13]Bowers, C. A. (1995). *Educating for an ecologically sustainable culture: Rethinking moral education, creativity, intelligence, and other modern orthodoxies.* Albany: State University of New York Press; Bowers, C. A. (1993). *Educational, cultural myths, and the ecological crisis: Toward deep changes.* Albany: State University of New York Press.

[14]Smith, G. A. (1992). *Education and the environment: Learning to live with limits.* Albany: State University of New York Press.

[15]Traina, F., & Darley-Hill, S. (Eds.) (1995). *Perspectives in bioregional education.* Troy, OH: North American Association for Environmental Education.

[16]Winters, W. G. (1993). *African American mothers and urban schools: The power of participation.* New York: Lexington.

[17]Cornbleth, C. (1990). *Curriculum in context.* (pp. 120–121 passim). New York: Falmer Press; Spring, J. (1996). *American education,* (7th ed.). New York: McGraw-Hill; Mercier, R. (1996). The greening of organizations. *Administration and Society, 27,* 459–472; Bolman, L. G., & Deal, T. E. (1992). *Reframing organizations: Artistry, choice, and leadership.* San Francisco: Jossey-Bass; Zeichner, K. (1991). Contradictions and tensions on the professionalization of teaching and the democratization of … *Teachers College Record, 92,* 363–374; Sergiovanni, T., & Corbally, J. (Eds.). (1984). *Leadership and organizational culture.* Urbana: University of Illinois Press; Smith, G. A. (1994). Preparing teachers to restructure schools. *Journal of Teacher Education, 45,* 18–30; Smyth, John. (Ed.). (1993). *A socially critical view of the self-managed school.* Washington, DC: Falmer Press; Foster, W. P. (1986). *Paradigms and prom-*

ises: New approaches to educational administration. Buffalo, NY: Prometheus.

[18]This exercise has been inspired by some of the classroom assignments and discussions developed by Profs. Fritz Mengert and Kathleen Casey, College of Education, University of North Carolina at Greensboro.

[19]Eckert, P. (1989). *Jocks and burnouts: Social categories and identity in high school.* New York: Teachers College Press; McLaren, P. (1989). *Life in schools: An introduction to critical pedagogy in the foundations of education.* New York: Longman; Van Berkun, D. W. (1995). The classroom with the empowered student. In M. Richardson, K. Lane, & J. Flanigan (Eds.), *School empowerment.* (pp. 277–288). Lancaster, PA: Technomic Publishing Company.

[20]Van Berkum, D. W. (1995). The classroom with the empowered student. In M. Richardson, K. Lane, & J. Flanigan (Eds.) *School empowerment* (pp. 277–288). Lancaster, PA: Technomic Publishing Company.

[21]LaMorte, M. (1996). *School law: Cases and concepts.* (pp. 84–188 passim.). Boston: Allyn & Bacon.

[22]Sergiovanni, T. J. (1991). *Moral leadership: Getting to the heart of school improvement.* San Francisco: Jossey-Bass; Shor, I. (1992). *Empowering education: Critical teaching for social change.* Chicago: University of Chicago Press; Smyth, J. (1991). *Teachers as collaborative learners: Challenging dominant forms of supervision.* Philadelphia: Open University Press.

[23]LaMorte, M. (1996). *School law: Cases and concepts.* (pp. 189–283 passim.). Boston: Allyn & Bacon.

[24]Hays, S. P. (1964). The politics of reform in municipal government in the Progressive Era. *Pacific Northwest Quarterly,* 55, October, pp. 157–169; Russo, C. J. (1992). The legal status of school boards in the intergovernmental system. In P. First & H. Walberg (Eds.), *School boards: Changing local control* (pp. 3–18). Berkeley, CA: McCutcheon; Spring, J. (1996). Local control, choice, charter schools, and privitization. In *American Education.* (7th ed) (pp. 171–192). New York: McGraw-Hill.

[25]Institute for Educational Leadership. (1986). *School boards: Strengthening grass roots leadership.* Washington, DC: IEL.

[26]Chart completely reconfigures that developed by Institute for Educational Leadership, *op.cit.,* 4.

[27]Spivak, H. S. (1973). *School decentralization and community control: Policy in search of a research agenda.* Boston: Institute for Responsive Education.

[28]Grant, C. (Ed.). (1979). *Community participation in education.* Boston: Allyn & Bacon; Medgley, C., & Woods, S. (1993). Beyond site-based management: Empowering teachers to reform schools. *Phi Delta Kappan,* 75, 245–252; Smith, G. (1994). Preparing teachers to restructure schools. *Journal of Teacher Education,* 45, 18–30; Wood, G. (1986). Action for democratic education. *Issues in Education,* 4,(3), Winter, 287–300.

[29]Katz, M. (1968). *The irony of early school reform.* Cambridge, MA: Harvard University Press.

[30]Comer, J.P. (1980). *Schoolpower: Implications of an intervention project.* New York: The Free Press; Epstein, J. L. (1986). *Toward an integrated theory of family–school connections.* Report No. 3. Baltimore: Center for Research on Elementary and Middle Schools, November; Fagnano. C. L., & Werber, B. Z. (Eds.) (1994). *School. family. and community interaction: A view from the firing lines.* Boulder, CO: Westview Press; Henderson, A.T. (1987). *The evidence continues to grow: Parent involvement improves education.* Columbia, MD: National Coalition of Citizens in Education; Herrick, S.C., & Epstein, J.L. (1991). *Improving school and family partnerships in urban elementary schools: Reading activity packets and school newsletters.* CDS Report No. 19., August.; Reglin, G. L. (1993). *At-risk "parent and family" involvement: Strategies for low income families of unmotivated and under-achieving students.* Springfield, IL: Charles C Thomas Publications; Ryan, B. A., Adams, G. R., Gullotta, T. P., Weissberg, R., & Hampton, L. (Eds.) (1995). *The family- school connection: Theory. research. and practice.* Thousand Oaks, CA: Sage; Winters, W. C. (1993). *African Ameri-*

can mothers and urban schools.: The power of participation New York: Lexington.

[31]Henderson, A., cited in Nieto, 1992, *Affirming Diversity: The sociopolitical context of multicultural education*. New York: Longman, p. 81.

[32]Henderson, A., Marburger, C., & Ooms, T. (Eds.), (1986). *Beyond the bake sale: An educator's guide to working with parents*. Washington, DC: National Committee for Citizens in Education, pp. 85–90.

[33]Epstein, J. L. (1986, November). *Toward an integrated theory of family–school connections*. Report No. 3, Baltimore: Center for Research on Elementary and Middle Schools.

[34]Comer, J. P. (1980). *Schoolpower: Implications of an intervention project*. New York: The Free Press; Epstein, J. L. (1986, November). *Toward an integrated theory of family–school connections*. Report No. 3, Baltimore: Center for Research on Elementary and Middle Schools. Epstein, J. L., & Dauber, S. L. (1989). *Teacher attitudes and practices of parent involvement in inner-city elementary and middle schools*. Report 33. Baltimore, MD: Center for Research on Elementary and Middle Schools, Johns Hopkins University; Fagnano. C. L., & Werber, B. Z., (Eds.) (1994). *School. family and community interaction: A view from the firing lines*. Boulder, CO: Westview Press; Henderson, A. T. (1987). *The evidence continues to grow: Parent involvement improves student achievement*. Columbia, MD: National Coalition of Citizens in Education; Reglin, G. L. (1993). *At-risk "parent and family" involvement: Strategies for low income families of unmotivated and underachieving students*. Springfield, IL: Charles C Thomas; Ryan, B. A., Adams, G. R., Gullotta, T. P., & Hampton, L. (Eds.) (1995). *The family–school connection: Theory. research. and practice*. Thousand Oaks, CA: Sage; Winters, W. C. (1993). *African American mothers and urban schools.: The power of participation*. New York: Lexington.

[35]Herrick, S. C., & Epstein, J. L. (1991). *Improving school and family partnerships in urban elementary schools: Reading activity packets and school newsletters. CDS Report No. 19*, August.

[36]Menacker, J., Hurwitz, E., & Weldom, W. 1988; cited in Fagnano. C. L., & Werber, B. Z.,

(Eds.) (1994). *School. family. and community interaction: A view from the firing lines*. Boulder, CO: Westview Press;

[37]Henderson, A., Marburger, C., & Ooms, T. (Eds.). (1986). *Beyond the bake sale: An educator's guide to working with parents*. Washington, DC: National Committee for Citizens in Education, pp. 91–93.

[38]National Commission on Excellence in Education. (1983). *A nation at risk*. Washington, DC: U.S. Governmental Printing Office.

[39]Epstein, J. L. (1986, November). *Toward an integrated theory of family–school connections*. Report No. 3, Baltimore: Center for Research on Elementary and Middle Schools.

[40]Martin, J. R. (1995). *The Schoolhome: Rethinking schools for changing families*. Cambridge, MA: Harvard University Press.

[41]Commission on Work, Family, and Citizenship. (1988) *The forgotten half: Non-college youth in America. An interim report*. Washington, DC: William T. Grant Foundation; Johnston, W. B., & Packer, A. H. (1987). *Work force 2000: Work and workers in the 21 st century*. Indianapolis, IN: Hudson Institute; Klerman, J., & Karoly, L. (1995). *The transition to stable employment: The experience of U.S. youth in their early labor market career*. Berkeley, CA: RAND Institute/NCRVE; Law, C. J., Knuth, R. A., & Bergman, S. (1992). What does the research say about school-to-work transition? Oak Brook, IL: NCREL, WWW NCREL Homepage; National Center on Education and the Economy. (1990). *America's choice: High skills or low wages! The report of the commission on the skills of the America's laborforce*. Rochester, NY: Author; Stern, D., & Eichorn, D. (1989). *Adolescence and work: Influences on social structure. labor markets. and culture*. Hillsdale, NJ: Lawrence Erlbaum Associates.

[42]Stern, D., Finkelstein, N., Stone, J., Latting, J., & Dornsife, C. (1995). *School to work: Research on programs in the United States*. Washington, DC: Falmer Press, p. 9.

[43]Ibid.

[44]Lakes, R. D. (Ed.) (1994). *Critical education and work: Multidisciplinary approaches*. Norwood, NJ: Ablex; Violas, P. (1978). *The training of the urban working class: A history of*

twentieth century American education. Chicago: Rand McNally College Publishing Company.

[45]Etizoni, A. (1993). *The spirit of community: The reinvention of American society.* New York: Simon & Schuster, p. 110.

[46]Ibid.

[47]Lakes, R. D. (Ed.) (1994). *Critical education and work: Multidisciplinary approaches.* Norwood, NJ: Ablex.

[48]This chart was suggested by information found in two sources: Law, C. J., Knuth, R. A. & Bergman, S. (1992). What does the research say about school-to-work transition? (pp. 12–13). Oak Brook, IL: NCREL, (WWW, NCREL Homepage) and Lakes, R. (Ed.) 1994. op. cit. (p. 167).

[49]Lakes, R. D. (Ed.) (1994). *Critical education and work: Multidisciplinary approaches.* Norwood, NJ: Ablex.

[50]O-Hanlon, T. (1980, Spring). Interscholastic athletics, 1900–1940: Shaping citizens for unequal roles in the modern industrial state. *Educational Theory,* 30:2.

[51]Spring, J. (1972). *Education and the rise of the corporate liberal state.* Boston: Beacon Press.

[52]Violas, P. (1978). *The training of the urban working class: A history of twentieth century American education.* Chicago: Rand McNally College Publishing Company.

[53]Sedlak, M., Wheeler, C., Pullin, D., & Cusick, P. (1986). Student employment and extracurricular sports. In *Selling students short: Classroom bargains and academic reform in the American high school* (pp. 59–68). New York: Teachers College Press.

[54]Spring, J. (1972). *Education and the rise of the corporate liberal state.* Boston: Beacon Press.

[55]Larkin, R. W. (1979). *Suburban youth in cultural crisis.* New York: Oxford University Press.

[56]Stern, D., & Eichorn, D. (Eds.) (1989). *Adolescence and work: Influences on social structure. labor markets. and culture.* Hillsdale, NJ: Lawrence Erlbaum Associates.

[57]Lewin-Epstein, N. (1981). *Youth employment during high school: An analysis of high school and beyond: A national longitudinal study for the 80s.* Chicago, IL: National Longitudinal

Center for Educational Statistics; National Association of Secondary School Principals. (1984). *The mood of American youth.* Reston, VA: Author: Nieto, S. (1992). *Affirming diversity: The sociopolitical context of multicultural education.* New York: Longman; Sedlak, M., Wheeler, C., Pullin, D., & Cusick, P. (1986). Student employment and extracurricular sports. In *Selling students short: Classroom bargains and academic reform in the American high school* (pp. 59–68). New York: Teachers College Press.

[58]Bennett, K., & LeCompte, M. D. (1995). *The way schools work: A sociological analysis of education.* New York: Longman; Gamoran, A., & Berends, M. (1987). The effects of stratification in secondary schools: A synthesis of survey and ethnographic research, *Review of Educational Research,* 57, 415–437.

[59]Webb, R., & Sherman, R. (1989). *Schooling and society.* New York: Macmillan, p. 307.

[60]Goffman, E. (1961). *Asylums.* (p. 304); cited in Webb, R., & Sherman, R. (1989). *op. cit.* p. 311.

[61]The chart "Observing 'Making Do' Classroom Situations" is based on research presented in R. Webb & R. Sherman (1989) *Schooling and society.* New York: Macmillan, pp. 311—319, passim.

[62]Merva, M., & Fowles, R. (1992). *Effects of diminished economic opportunities on social stress: Heart attacks. strokes. and crime.* Washington, DC: Economic Policy Institute, pp. 1–2.

[63]Rifkin, J. (1995). *The end of work: The decline of the global labor force and the dawn of the post-market era.* New York: Putnam.

[64]Ibid.

[65]Burbach, H. (1995). Violence and the public schools. Curry School of Education, University of Virginia, WWW site; Rifkin, J. (1995). The end of work: The decline of the global *labor force and the dawn of the post-market era.* New York: Putnam, pp. 209–210.

[66]Anderson, C. S. (1982). The search for school climate: A review of the research. *Review of Educational Research* 52, 368–420; Brown, D. (1994). Youth violence: Causes and solutions. *Thrust for Educational Leadership* 24, 10; Garcia, P. (1994). Creating a safe school climate, *Thrust for Educational Leadership.* 24, 22.

[67]Rifkin, J. (1995). *The end of work: The decline of the global labor force and the dawn of the post-market era.* New York: Putnam, p. 210.

[68]Brown, D. (1994). Youth violence: Causes and solutions. *Thrust for Educational Leadership, 24,* 10; Garcia, P. (1994). Creating a safe school climate, *Thrust for Educational Leadership. 24,* 22; Rifkin, J. (1995). *The end of work: The decline of the global labor force and the dawn of the post-market era.* New York: Putnam; National School Board Association. (1994). *Violence in our schools: How America's school boards are safeguarding your children.* Washington, DC: Author; Squires, D. A., Huit, W. G., & Segars, J. K. (1983). Effective schools and classrooms: A *research-based perspective.* Alexandria, MA: ASCD; Vestermark, S. D., & Blauvelt, P. (1978). *Controlling crime in school: A complete security handbook for administrators.* West Nyack, NY: Parker Publishing Company

[69]National Institute of Education. (1978). *Violent schools—safe schools: The safe school study report to Congress. Volume I.* Washington, DC: Government Printing Office.

[70]National Institute of Education. (1978). *Violent schools—safe schools: The safe school study report to Congress. Volume I.* Washington, DC: Government Printing Office; Hill, M. S., & Hill, F. W. (1994). *Creating safe schools: What principals can do.* Thousand Oaks, CA: Corwin Press.

[71]Benedickt, M. (Ed.) (1991). *Cyberspace: First steps.* Cambridge, MA: MIT Press; Herring, S. C. (1993). Gender and democracy in computer-mediated communication, *Electronic Journal of Communication* 3,2.

[72]Gergen, K. J. (1991). *The saturated self.* New York: Basic Books; Jones, S. (Ed.) (1995). *Cybersociety: Computer-mediated communication and community.* Thousand Oaks, CA: Sage; Kramarae, C. (Ed.) (1991). *Technology and women's voices.* New York: Routledge & Kegan Paul; Turkle, S. (1984). *The second self: Computers and the human spirit.* New York: Simon & Schuster; Turkle, S. (1995). *Life on the screen; Identity in the age of the Internet.* New York: Simon & Schuster.

[73]Reingold, H. (1993). *The virtual community: Homesteading on the electronic frontier.* Reading, MA: Addison-Wesley.

[74]Ibid.

[75]Kapor, M. (1995). Mind on-line: The first noble truth. Electronic document. WWW: Mitchell Kapor Homepage at Electronic Frontier Foundation Internet Homepage.

Section 5

After the Field Experience: Now What?

REDESIGNING THE CURRICULUM

Background

Talking about curriculum is like talking about the ocean: The topic is huge and everybody's perspective is different. Some view curriculum only as the official course of study offered by a school or system of schools. Others see curriculum as including both the official course of study and the hidden, or excluded, knowledge. Although these perspectives are different, they share a common denominator of defining curriculum as content.

There are others who define curriculum in a much broader sense. These individuals understand curriculum as the total package of training that students receive in schools. For these individuals, curriculum exists at multiple levels of openness and awareness. This approach to curriculum also includes what some call "the affective," that is, the transmission of ideology and culturally bound forms of knowledge and action.

There are yet others who define curriculum as existing in all aspects of daily living, including the schools. They would argue that television and popular media are powerful curricular models that are very effective forms of teaching under the guise of entertainment, news, information, and so forth. For these individuals, the formal curriculum of schooling is only one small slice of the teaching and learning that occurs every day in our society.

Where, then, do we begin? For the purposes of this section, let us construct a double continuum of curriculum. The x axis represents the range of content to context. That is, on one end we will restrict ourselves to envisioning curricu-lum as only the formal content of what we teach—the course of study. On the other end is context. According to this view, curriculum encompasses the wide range of social experiences, structures, and forms, and is a powerful and always present part of our daily lives in or out of school. The y axis is the continuum from school to society at large. This considers where curriculum resides. On one extreme, the existence of curriculum is limited only to the school setting. On the other, curriculum is present throughout all social landscapes.

Here, then, in the following diagram is what we have so far. Remember the x and y axes represent continua, not polar opposites.

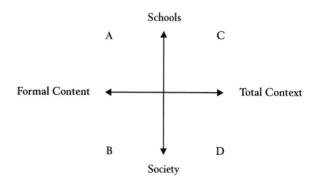

Most of the mainstream work in curriculum reform has taken place in the A and C quadrants. These are the areas that limit the definition of curriculum to the formal content or the course of study for a school or a school system. Frankly, this is also the most easily managed area for thinking about curriculum. Most teachers and education workers place their personal definitions of curriculum within these two quadrants largely because that is how most colleges and universities teach teachers to think about curriculum.

Activity

There have been literally hundreds, if not thousands, of books written in this country in the last century about curriculum and curriculum redesign. We obviously will not try to tackle a subject of such oceanic proportions in one exercise. What we propose is that you go back and review some of your reflective narrative notes and consider additional questions. Hopefully, these questions will position you in such a way as to touch on the breadth of curriculum thought: in other words, all four quadrants.

1. *Cultural portrait.* You were asked to consider the nature of your assumptions about other people. How has the content of the formal curriculum helped to shape those assumptions? How might we redesign curricular content to present a more accurate representation of various groups and cultures? Which groups seem to be largely present or missing in the curriculum at large? Think about both the formal curriculum and the manner in which schools are organized (i.e., how schools teach one to act and behave). How might we redesign the way we "do schooling" to be more open and inclusive for all groups?

2. *Historical linkages to contemporary practices.* How much of the curriculum content exists simply because of tradition? Does this content have a place or fill a need in our contemporary world? How might we go about evaluating whether or not traditional content is appropriate in the present? How much of school organization, policy, and practice is based on traditional models or organization? What lessons are taught through these forms? How might we redesign these forms so that the lessons are more appropriate to life in a democratic society?

3. *Textbook analysis.* How current or accurate are the texts you reviewed? Are there ways of redesigning the curriculum to make knowledge more appropriate to contemporary and individual needs? Textbooks are largely controlled by publishing houses, state legislatures, and special interest groups. How might the curriculum be redesigned to break this monopoly of power and involve the students and community in the production of knowledge? How might we begin to

use and interrogate the larger cultural forms in society (i.e., music, television, films, etc.) as a form of curriculum?

4. *What counts as knowledge?* How might we redesign the curriculum to include various forms of knowledge? What criteria might be used to decide which knowledge should be official and which unofficial?

RETHINKING STUDENT–TEACHER RELATIONSHIPS AND LEARNING

Background

We all know that learning is not a one-way activity from teacher to student. Yet, for the most part, we continue to plan lessons in schools as if students were empty vessels waiting to be filled with facts. Most lesson plans, especially at the middle and secondary level, continue to adopt a lecture format, encouraging students to be passive in the educational process. Students become proficient at this form of schooling in which they are not held responsible for organizing their own learning.

Such education perpetuates the feeling that what happens in school either has nothing to do with real life, or at best is just a preparation for the real world. Thus, students are often dis-abled in their learning, instead of becoming empowered and enabled. The curiosity that young children exhibit is stifled in the schools. One major challenge facing educators today is the quest to rekindle this curiosity in order to support the natural curiosity of learners.

How might educators address this problem? Perhaps the relationship between teachers and students can be changed so that learners are encouraged to take a larger role in their own education. How might the fact that teachers are also learners help in alleviating this one-sidedness in schools? How might we redefine learning to encourage a higher level of life-long learning for everyone in our society? The following activity encourages you to address these concerns.

Activity

Brainstorm about this topic with friends and relatives. Return to your notes and comments that were stimulated by the Reflective Narrative sections of the following activities. Use these notes to guide you in the process of rethinking student–teacher relationships and learning.

1. Classroom characteristics and climate. How does the teacher's authoritative style (e.g., autocratic or democratic) affect teacher–student relationships? Which climate did you identify as more effective? Thinking now about how students and teachers relate to one another, do you still find this position more effective? These positions represent two extremes. What other positions can you articulate as alternatives?

2. *Learning activities.* What links did you make between the activities of particular classrooms and the supposed ability level of the students? What can the activities required of teachers by students tell you about the nature of their relationship? Let these responses guide you in brainstorming about the kinds of activities that you believe enhance student–teacher relationships versus those that cause these relationships to deteriorate.

3. *Brain-compatible classrooms.* This activity considers stress generated in classrooms. Review your responses to these questions, and turn your attention to how tension and stress affects teacher–student relationships? Again, at what point does a challenging environment lead to a distant relationship?

4. *Student governance and decision making.* How do student governance issues affect teacher–student relationships? Do governing organizations empower students (all students, some students, which students and in what ways)? Do some students become disempowered through involvement or exclusion from these organizations? Keep these issues in mind as you rethink these relationships.

Review your responses to the Reflective Narratives from other activities that you have completed. Glean as much information from these reflections as possible to guide you in your exploration of possible student–teacher relationships. Then record your findings (write a list, make a video or audio tape, etc.). Finally, for each of the discoveries or suggestions you make, generate at least one thing you can do to bring this vision into existence.

REDESIGNING CLASSROOMS

Background

One of the most common assumptions about education is that it must take place in classrooms. Traditionally, we think of classrooms as having four walls, a chalkboard at the front, a teacher's desk in front or back, students' desks arranged in rows, and perhaps a window or two. This exercise challenges you to think beyond this traditional stereotype to generate creative possibilities.

Why must we assume that learning occurs best when students are seated in plastic or wooden desks arranged in straight rows? Is there any reason to believe that staring at the back of another student's head is conducive to learning? Why should students sit at uncomfortable desks instead of on chairs with cushions?

Activity

Recall the questions raised by some of the exercises encountered earlier in this book. On the basis of your own recent observations as well as your prior experiences in school, think about how you might redesign classrooms. Look back at the Reflective Narrative sections of the following exercises for guidance.

1. *Finding a sense of place.* What were the essential features of your special place? How can classroom environments be altered to include these features? What would such a learning environment look like? You might want to make a sketch or drawing of your space.

2. *Metaphors of classroom praxis.* What metaphors did you explore in this exercise? How did these metaphors change the way you think about schools? Use one or more of the metaphors in this exercise to help you think differently about how classrooms are designed.

3. *Historical linkages to classroom practice.* Recall your investigation of the historic tradition of particular classroom practices. How might your observations and suggestions here relate to redesigning classrooms? If, for example, you believe that certain practices should be modified,

how might this modification lead to redesigned classrooms?

4. *Sick building–classroom syndrome.* Here you were asked to think about the relationship of design to the teaching–learning process. What suggestions did you offer here. How can you implement and include these changes in your classroom design?

Stretch your imagination beyond what you are accustomed to thinking of as a classroom and think about the places, the settings, and the times when you enjoy learning. Brainstorm about how you might redesign classrooms. Explore a variety of labels for classrooms (the metaphors exercise may help here). Think perhaps about outdoor learning centers, educational facilities or nearby corporate buildings, study or quiet areas, and other names that help you expand possibilities for classrooms. Make a list of various possibilities. Make a sketch, paint a picture, or even construct a model of a classroom as you might redesign it.

REDESIGNING TEACHER EDUCATION

Background

In the aftermath of the publication of *A Nation Prepared: Teachers for the 21st Century*, a highly critical report of how colleges and universities were preparing preservice teachers, numerous teacher training programs throughout the United States began making substantial changes in their teacher preparation programs. Many of these changes have resulted in organized reform groups. For example, the Holmes Group, consisting primarily of deans of education at major research universities, promotes the idea of preservice teachers earning a bachelor's degree in liberal arts and a master's degree in education. Similarly, the Project 30 Alliance advocates the addition of more liberal arts courses to teacher preparation. The Renaissance Group, composed primarily of universities that were once teacher-training colleges, asserts that teacher training should begin early in one's university career and that preservice teachers should have extensive experience in the field before student teaching.

The National Network for Educational Renewal, founded by John Goodland, believes that reform in public education must go hand in hand with reform in teacher education. Following the footsteps of the National Network for Educational Renewal, the state of Georgia has adopted the P-16 initiative that calls for co-reform between public education and teacher education programs.

Activities

1. Evaluate your own teacher education program. What courses are mandatory for all education majors? Why do you think these courses are mandatory? When do field experiences begin in your program? How much time do you think prospective teachers should spend in classrooms observing, teaching lessons, tutoring students, and so on.

2. Is your teacher preparation program part of any of the preceding reform initiatives? Find out what changes your state has made in teacher certification in the last 5 years. What precipiated these changes?

3. Interview teachers who graduated from your teacher training program within the last 3 years. How well did their university work prepare them for their jobs? What suggestions do they have about reforming teacher education?

4. With a group, brainstorm your responses to the following and the implications for teacher education: Can prospective teachers be taught sensitivity? Can we promote emotional, moral, and spiritual intelligence through teacher education programs? What role can teacher education programs serve in encouraging teachers to develop the self that will inspire our children to become better people?

5. As a group project, rewrite your teacher education program in a way that you feel will best prepare preservice teachers to teach in the schools of the 21st century. Include in your discussion whether the bulk of your courses should be taken in the College of Education or in other colleges on your campus (e.g., College of Liberal Arts). Also, include whether the teacher program should be a 4-year or 5-year program.

Index

A

Authority, 15, 42, 55, 57, 89, 91

B

Bioregionalism, 93
Brain, 48, 57, 65–66, 87, 147

C

Community, vii, xi–xiv, 15, 23–24, 37, 49, 89–93,
    102–103, 107, 110, 114–115, 123, 126, 134,
    137–139, 141–142, 146
Control, x–xiii, xv, 15–19, 21, 25–28, 31, 41, 44,
    57–58, 75, 86, 89, 91–93, 99–101, 103–104,
    107–110, 137, 139–140
Culture, vii, ix–xvi, 1–2, 5–6, 9–11, 13, 20, 25–30,
    33, 35–37, 47–49, 51–52, 55, 59, 73, 86,
    89–91, 93, 96, 99–103, 111, 114, 118–119,
    122, 125–126, 129–130, 133–134, 139,
    141–142, 146
Curriculum, ix–xi, xvi, 6, 9–10, 31, 33, 39–40, 47–48,
    55–59, 66, 70, 87, 90, 92, 95–101, 105, 107,
    109, 112, 118, 122–127, 139–140, 145–146
Cyberspace, 92, 137–138, 142

D

Deculturalization, xvi
Democratic, x, 49, 75–76, 89, 91–93, 100, 102–103,
    137, 139, 141, 146–147
Dialogue, vii, ix, xii, 12, 48–49, 67–71, 101, 137
Discourse, xi, xv, 27–28, 90–92, 137
Dress codes, xv, 16–17, 27, 29, 31, 35–36, 39–40, 134

E

Ecology model, 134
Ecosystem, xv–xvi, 89
Empowerment, 7, 11, 91–93, 99–102, 104, 107–108,
    117, 140
Extracurricular activities, 107

F

Faculty governance, 101
Female body, 17, 27

G

Gender, vii, ix–x, xiv–xv, 1–2, 6, 9–11, 19–20, 27–28,
    33, 43–44, 47, 55, 61–62, 73, 85–86, 97,
    114–115, 125–126, 130, 138, 142

H

Hegemony, ix–x, 18
Hidden curriculum, 48, 57, 87, 97
History, xv–xvi, 47, 53–55, 93, 98, 101, 111,
    125–126, 139, 141–142

I

Ideology, ix–xiv, 33, 40, 48, 58, 87, 92–93, 96–97, 145
Ideology of schooling, xi
Ideology, dominant, xi
Images, 54, 89–93, 96–98, 119

K

Knowing, vii, 1, 5, 53
Knowledge, vii, ix–xi, xiv, 1, 41, 45, 47–49, 53, 55,
    57–59, 83, 122, 137, 145–146

L

Local control, 91, 104, 140

M

Mainstreaming, 109
Male body, 17, 29
Meaning, viii, xv, 7, 49
Metaphors, x, xv, 42, 89–93, 95–96, 147–148
Moral messages, 48, 59–60
Multicultural, xvi, 1–2, 9, 11, 52, 57–58, 61–62, 142

N

National standards, 92, 103
Null curriculum, xi

P

Parent participation, 105, 119
Parent–teacher relationships, 117
Pedagogy, ix–xi, xv–xvi, 3–4, 12–13, 31, 47, 55–56,
    61–62, 65, 70, 79–80, 87, 96, 99, 108, 122,
    139–140